Toward Country-led Development

A Multi-Partner Evaluation of the Comprehensive Development Framework

Synthesis
Report

This evaluation has been supported and guided by the following organizations and countries, which form its Steering Committee.

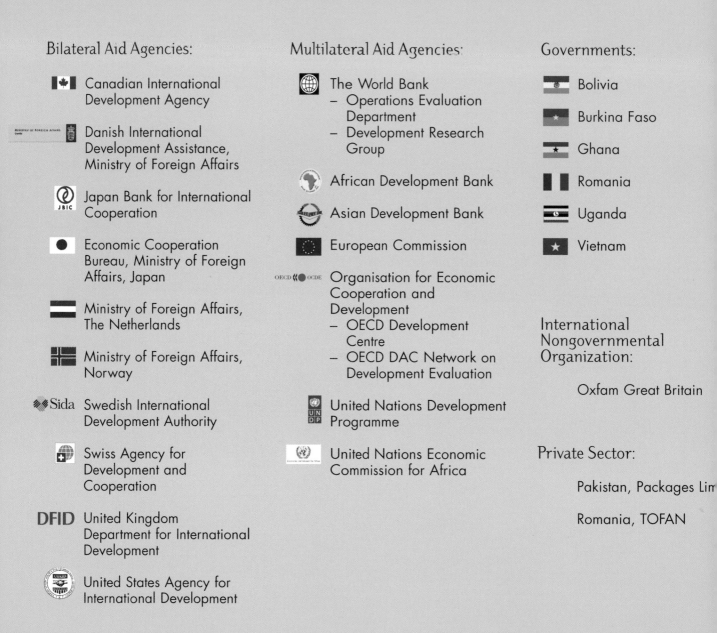

Bilateral Aid Agencies:

- Canadian International Development Agency
- Danish International Development Assistance, Ministry of Foreign Affairs
- Japan Bank for International Cooperation
- Economic Cooperation Bureau, Ministry of Foreign Affairs, Japan
- Ministry of Foreign Affairs, The Netherlands
- Ministry of Foreign Affairs, Norway
- Swedish International Development Authority
- Swiss Agency for Development and Cooperation
- United Kingdom Department for International Development
- United States Agency for International Development

Multilateral Aid Agencies:

- The World Bank
  - Operations Evaluation Department
  - Development Research Group
- African Development Bank
- Asian Development Bank
- European Commission
- Organisation for Economic Cooperation and Development
  - OECD Development Centre
  - OECD DAC Network on Development Evaluation
- United Nations Development Programme
- United Nations Economic Commission for Africa

Governments:

- Bolivia
- Burkina Faso
- Ghana
- Romania
- Uganda
- Vietnam

International Nongovernmental Organization:

Oxfam Great Britain

Private Sector:

Pakistan, Packages Lim

Romania, TOFAN

Toward Country-led Development

A Multi-Partner Evaluation of the
Comprehensive Development Framework

Synthesis
Report

Contents

Foreword

We have had the challenge and the responsibility of overseeing the implementation of a large, complex, and unique evaluative effort. The undertaking was remarkable in several respects:

▪ The *governance structure* involved some 30 stakeholders from partner countries, donors and development agencies, and from an international NGO and a private sector enterprise.

▪ The *11 component studies* were conducted by teams composed of evaluators and researchers intentionally drawn from the South and the North.

▪ A multi-partner *Management Group* drawn from the Steering Committee oversaw the day-to-day work of the secretariat and the progress of the evaluation.

▪ *Ten donors* provided financial or in-kind support for the evaluation.

None of these elements is unprecedented by itself, but we believe the combination is unparalleled. The effort generated valuable experience in collaborative evaluation of development issues and provided an unusually broad perspective and solid support for the resulting conclusions and recommendations. We believe that the recommendations, if adopted by donors and countries, will result not only in more widespread adoption of the principles of the Comprehensive Development Framework, but also in sustained progress in reducing poverty on a larger scale.

CDF Evaluation Management Group

Gregory K. Ingram, Co-Chair
Director-General
Operations Evaluation, World Bank

Paul Collier, Co-Chair
Director
Development Research Group, World Bank

Marcelo Barron
External Finance General Directorate
Ministry of Finance, Bolivia

Emmanuel Tumusiime-Mutebile
Governor
Bank of Uganda

Niels Dabelstein
Head, Danida Evaluation Secretariat
Ministry of Foreign Affairs, Denmark

Preface

The Comprehensive Development Framework—launched by World Bank President James D. Wolfensohn in early 1999—has become an important influence on the global development agenda. It provided conceptual underpinnings for the Poverty Reduction Strategy Papers (PRSPs) and fed into such initiatives as the Millennium Development Goals (MDGs) and the Monterrey Consensus. The core Comprehensive Development Framework (CDF) principles have gained widespread endorsement. They are not new individually, but bringing them together as a unified concept and championing the package within the global development community has been an important innovation.

This report concludes an extended multi-partner effort to evaluate the implementation of the CDF principles, to identify the factors that have facilitated and hindered it, and to assess the extent to which CDF implementation has affected behaviors and outcomes. The breadth of the evaluation's multi-partner approach and governance structure has been virtually unprecedented, and the process itself generated valuable experience on collaborative ways to evaluate issues of broad mutual interest to the development community.

The evaluation has its origins in a December 1999 request by the Bank's Board Committee on Development Effectiveness (CODE) to the Operations Evaluation Department (OED) to assess CDF implementation. OED and the Bank's Development Economics Research Group (DECRG) joined forces and launched the evaluation by hosting a conference with representatives from CDF pilot countries, donors, nongovernmental and private sector organizations, and academia. This group recommended that the evaluation should be a multi-stakeholder partnership. Accordingly, a 30-member Steering Committee and 5-member Management Group were established in January 2001 to guide the evaluation. Multi-disciplinary evaluation teams with members from developed and developing countries conducted six country studies and five thematic studies. Nine bilateral and multilateral donors provided financial and in-kind support, amounting to about 60 percent of the evaluation's total cost.

The evaluation shows that both donors and recipients have made progress in implementing the CDF principles, particularly in countries where one or more of the principles have been applied over a number of years. These positive changes are fragile and could be stalled or reversed. Implementing the principles requires changes in entrenched behaviors and institutional practices—not easily or quickly done. Thus, dedicated and consistent attention is needed by top donor leadership and recipient countries to ensure that momentum is sustained.

Acknowledgments

A 30-member, multi-partner steering committee and a 5-member management group have governed the CDF evaluation.

Management Group

Gregory K. Ingram (co-chair), *Director-General, Operations Evaluation, World Bank.*

Paul Collier (co-chair), *Director, Development Research Group, World Bank.*

Marianela Zeballos, *General Director,* and Marcelo Barron, *General Directorate for External Finance, Bolivia.*

Niels Dabelstein, *Director, Evaluation Secretariat, Danish International Development Agency, Ministry of Foreign Affairs, Denmark*

Emmanuel Tumusiime-Mutebile, *Governor, Bank of Uganda.*

Financial Support

The World Bank and the governments of Canada, Denmark, the Netherlands, Norway, Sweden, Switzerland, and the United Kingdom provided financial support for the evaluation. The Asian Development Bank and Japan provided staff and consultant support for the Vietnam country case study.

Contributors

CDF Evaluation Secretariat: Ibrahim Elbadawi, Lead Economist, Development Research Group, World Bank, and John Eriksson, Task Team Leader, Operations Evaluation Department, World Bank, provided overall coordination for the evaluation. John Eriksson and Laura Kullenberg, Senior Evaluation Officer, Operations Evaluation Department, coordinated and edited the final report. They also led or coordinated the country case studies. Victoria Elliott, Operations Evaluation Department, World Bank, managed OED's contributions.

Chapter 1:
Carol Lancaster, *Associate Professor and Director, Masters of Science in Foreign Service, Foreign Service Program, Georgetown University*; Alison Scott, *Senior Social Development Adviser, Department for International Development, UK*; and Laura Kullenberg.

Chapter 2:
Paul Collier; Laura Kullenberg; Charles Soludo, *Professor of Economics, University of Nigeria, Nsukka*; Mirafe Marcos, *Research Analyst, Operations Evaluation Department*; and John Eriksson.

Chapter 3:
Paul Collier; Alison Scott; Ibrahim Elbadawi; John Randa, *Research Analyst, Development Research Group*; and John Eriksson.

Chapter 4:
CDF Evaluation Secretariat.

Advisers to the Report Drafting Team:

Hirohisa Kohama, *Professor of Economics, University of Shizuoka, Japan.*
Don Pressley, *Principal, Booz Allen Hamilton, Washington, D.C.*
Alison Scott, *Senior Social Development Adviser, Department for International Development, UK.*
Samuel Wangwe, *Executive Director, Economic and Social Research Foundation, Tanzania.*

In Addition:

Simon Maxwell, Director of the Overseas Development Institute, UK, provided comments on draft chapters of the report.

Mirafe Marcos and Georgia Wallen, Research Analysts, provided research support; in addition, Mirafe Marcos participated as a member of the Ghana and Uganda country case study teams.

William B. Hurlbut and Caroline McEuen, Writer/Editors, Operations Evaluation Department, provided technical support for document production and editing.

Julia Ooro, Program Assistant, provided administrative and document production and editing support.

Tourya Tourougui, Program Assistant, provided administrative support.

The volume was published in OED's Partnerships and Knowledge Group, under the direction of Osvaldo Feinstein, by the Outreach and Dissemination staff of the Knowledge Management Unit, including Patrick Grasso, Lead Knowledge Management Officer; Vivian Jackson, Publications Officer; Caroline McEuen, Writer/Editor; and Juicy Qureishi-Huq, Program Assistant.

A Development Expert Looks at the CDF Evaluation

Boiled down to its essentials, evaluation is about answering three questions: 'Does it work?' 'Is it worth it?', and 'Why?' The third question is often neglected.

Simon Maxwell
Director, Overseas Development Institute

Simon Maxwell applies his three evaluation criteria to the findings of this evaluation of the Comprehensive Development Framework. He identifies donors as most in need of "radical change" and ends with a heretical thought:

In the case of the CDF evaluation we learn that the four core principles of the CDF have largely been operationalized through the PRSP process, which similarly emphasizes (a) long-term and holistic vision, (b) country ownership, (c) results orientation, and (d) country-led partnership. We learn that none of these ideas is entirely new, but that the CDF/PRSP initiatives have helped to accelerate and reinforce adoption, albeit unevenly. We are led to conclude that there are practical benefits, especially in terms of more widely-owned and better-targeted public expenditure programs. And we can surmise that all this is worth it because progress towards the Millennium Development Goals will be faster than it would otherwise have been. A PRSP is not a perfect incarnation of the CDF principles, but it is a good start, it is worth it, and it does, up to a point, work.

There is still some way to go, however. Long-term visions are not always shared by competings political parties. Participatory processes can be—and sometimes are—aptured by vested interests. Results-based approaches are theoretically contested and hard to implement. And donors find it almost impossible to sustain genuine partnerships based on reciprocal accountability.

Asking 'why' performance falls short of the ideal—so far—points to what must happen next. First, expectations need to be realistic. For example, a national consensus on economic policy, sustained over time, is unachievable and probably undesirable. Second, implementation needs to be pragmatic. For example, the genuine problems with simplistic, target-driven approaches to the reform of public administration need to be recognized by adopting more flexible guidelines. Third, even pragmatic implementation takes time and needs resources, especially for capacity building. And finally, the incentives need to be right, both for recipient countries and within donor agencies.

The most radical change needed at present is by donors. There are some practical things they should do differently in-country, for example to reinforce the role of parliaments in policy-making. But more generally, a political commitment is needed, translated into rules, regulations and decisions about resource allocation, to simplify and harmonize procedures, coordinate policy dialogue, and improve accountability to recipient country stakeholders. A heretical thought: is not one way to do this to increase the share of multilateral rather than bilateral aid?

Abbreviations and Acronyms

ADB	Asian Development Bank
BPRS	Bolivia Poverty Reduction Strategy
CAF	Corporación Andina de Fomento
CAS	Country Assistance Strategy
CDF	Comprehensive Development Framework
CG	Consultative Group
CSLP	Cadre Stratégique de Lutte contre la Pauvreté
CODE	Committee on Development Effectiveness
CPIA	Country Policy and Institutional Assessment
CPRGS	Comprehensive Poverty Reduction and Growth Strategy
DAC	Development Assistance Committee
DEC	Development Economics (World Bank)
DECRG	Development Economics Research Group
DFID	Department for International Development
EBRD	European Bank for Reconstruction and Development
ESW	Economic and Sector Work
EC	European Commission
EU	European Union

GDP	Gross Domestic Product
GNI	Gross National Income
GoB	Government of Bolivia
GoV	Government of Vietnam
GPRA	Government Performance and Results Act
GPRS	Ghana Poverty Reduction Strategy
HIPC	Heavily Indebted Poor Countries
HQs	Headquarters
IDA	International Development Association
IDGs	International Development Goals
IFI	International Financial Institution
IMF	International Monetary Fund
I-PRSP	Interim Poverty Reduction Strategy Paper
JBIC	Japan Bank for International Cooperation
JSA	Joint Staff Assessment
LCR	Latin America and the Caribbean Region of the World Bank
LICUS	Low-Income Countries under Stress
M&E	Monitoring and Evaluation
MDB	Multilateral Development Bank
MDGs	Millennium Development Goals
MENA	Middle East and North Africa Region (World Bank)

MFPED	Ministry of Finance, Planning, and Economic Development (Uganda)	PRSC	Poverty Reduction Support Credit
MIT	Massachusetts Institute of Technology	PRSP	Poverty Reduction Strategy Paper
MOFA	Ministry of Foreign Affairs	RBM	Results-based Management
MTEF	Medium-term Expenditure Framework	SPA	Strategic Partnership with Africa
NEPAD	New Partnership for Africa's Development	SSA	Sub-Saharan Africa
NGO	Nongovernmental Organization	SWAp	Sectorwide Approach
NSSD	National Strategy for Sustainable Development	TA	Technical Assistance
ODA	Official Development Assistance	UK	United Kingdom
OECD	Organisation for Economic Cooperation and Development	UNDAF	United Nations Development Assistance Framework
OED	Operations Evaluation Department	UNDP	United Nations Development Programme
PAF	Poverty Action Fund	UNECA	United Nations Economic Commission for Africa
PEAP	Poverty Eradication Action Plan	UNICEF	United Nations Children's Fund
PIU	Project Implementation Unit	UPEI	Universal Primary Education Initiative
PPA	Participatory Poverty Assessment	US	United States
PREM	Poverty Reduction and Economic Management	USAID	United States Agency for International Development
PRGF	Poverty Reduction and Growth Facility	WG	Working Group

Executive Summary

This evaluation report synthesizes the findings of a multi-partner effort to assess implementation of the Comprehensive Development Framework (CDF). The evaluation's primary objectives are to:

- Identify the factors that have facilitated implementation of CDF principles, and those that have hindered it.

- Assess the extent to which CDF implementation has affected intermediate outcomes and, to the extent possible, longer-term development outcomes.

Background

In the mid-1990s, the aid community began a candid self-assessment. Disappointing development results—especially in Sub-Saharan Africa—had raised troubling questions: Does the emphasis on structural adjustment ignore the poor? Do the many agencies and international organizations working in developing countries overburden, rather than strengthen, the capacity of recipient governments? Does the poor coordination of donors add to the challenge of making development effective? Increasingly, the painful realization of development agencies, recipient countries, and aid analysts was "yes"—the full potential of international aid to reduce poverty by achieving positive, sustainable development results was not being fulfilled.

In response, the donor community took a number of steps, from debt relief through the joint World Bank-IMF Heavily Indebted Poor Countries (HIPC) initiative to shifting the aid focus from inputs to measurable outcomes, as with the *International Development Goals* promulgated by the OECD Development Assistance Committee. Recipient countries also began to develop remedies: the Vietnamese government urged donors to work together to reduce the administrative burdens of aid management, and Uganda adopted a long-term framework and a results-measurement approach for its poverty reduction efforts.

At the World Bank, these strands came together in 1998 in a Partnerships Group. Its purpose was announced by its name: to develop the concept of aid as a *partnership* between recipient governments and donors. This presaged the introduction in early 1999 of the Comprehensive Development Framework, which, as described by Bank President James Wolfensohn, was a new way for the Bank to do business with recipient countries and other development partners.

New Approaches Informed by Past Shortcomings

At the heart of the CDF is the belief that the way aid is delivered, not just its content, has an important influence on its effectiveness, and that poverty reduction is the fundamental goal of international aid. The CDF consists of four principles—a Long-Term, Holistic Development Framework; Results Orientation, Country Ownership; and Country-led Partnership—each of which responds to past development assistance shortcomings and presents an approach for improvement.

■ Development strategies should be comprehensive and holistic, and shaped by a long-term vision. Past emphasis on short-term macroeconomic stabilization and balance of payment pressures overwhelmed longer-term structural and social considerations (for example, expanding and improving education and health facilities, maintaining infrastructure, and training a new generation of public officials).

■ Development performance should be evaluated through measurable, on-the-ground results. The traditional emphasis on disbursement levels and project inputs has measured resource allocation and consumption. What really matters is impact on people and their needs.

■ Development goals and strategies should be "owned" by the country, based on citizen participation in shaping them. While donor-driven aid delivered under structural adjustment was sometimes effective, in many cases painful and lengthy adjustment measures were eventually undone. When countries have greater say in shaping reforms, governments and their citizens will be more committed to seeing them through.

■ Recipient countries should lead aid management and coordination through stakeholder partnerships. Partnerships built on transparency, mutual trust, and consultation can improve aid coordination and reduce the inefficiencies, asymmetrical power relationships, and tensions of donor-led aid initiatives.

In 1999, several countries volunteered to pilot CDF approaches. Many others soon developed broad-based Poverty Reduction Strategy Papers, or PRSPs, in order to access debt relief under the HIPC initiative. All four of the CDF principles served as the basis for PRSP development. Other donors and recipients also supported CDF tenets, which often reinforced their own inclinations or policies. And the CDF came to influence the way subsequent global initiatives, such as the Millennium Development Goals, have been framed.

"Why" and "How" of the Evaluation

In late 1999, the Bank's Executive Board Committee on Development Effectiveness asked OED to assess CDF implementation. OED joined forces with the Bank's Development Research Group to begin designing an evaluation approach. Then, in true CDF fashion, representatives of pilot countries, donor agencies, and civil society and private sector organizations argued that the evaluation should be conducted and governed along multi-partner lines. The resulting 30-member Steering Committee chose 5 members to serve as a Management Group.

Because the Steering Committee concluded early on that it was not yet possible to ascribe development outcomes directly to the CDF, the evaluation focuses on the extent to which CDF principles or *CDF-like* principles have been implemented in six case study countries— Bolivia, Burkina Faso, Ghana, Romania, Uganda, and Vietnam—and what the effects and implications have been thus far.

Multi-disciplinary evaluation teams, with members from developed and developing countries, conducted the country studies as well as thematic studies of each of the CDF principles. In addition, a quantitative study of 88 developing countries analyzed relationships between development outcome measures and proxy indicators of CDF-like development strategies. The evaluation focuses primarily on the relationship between recipient governments and donors and development agencies. The CDF principles cover all development relationships, including those among civil society and private sector partners.

Evaluation Conclusions and Recommendations

Four sets of conclusions and corresponding recommendations—reflecting the four CDF principles—emerged from the evaluation synthesis, with recommendations for recipient governments and the donor community, and, in some cases, additional recommendations addressed specifically to the World Bank. The evaluation also found that there can be tensions in how the CDF principles are applied, specifically involving ownership and partnership, and the long-term focus and the emphasis on results. These have been long-standing tensions in development practice and are neither novel nor unique to the CDF. There is also evidence at the country level that the CDF principles can be complementary. Country leadership, whether at the highest levels of government, in line ministries, or among elected officials, remains a critical factor for making and sustaining progress on each of the principles, and for ensuring complementarity among them as they are implemented.

The PRSP is a powerful tool for implementing the CDF principles in low-income countries, and on those grounds merits continued support and development. For the PRSP to succeed, it will need coherent and sustained external support, as well as a lengthy process of learning by doing. The ideal PRSP will not be produced and implemented overnight, but will require widespread public sector reform and institution building. These are long-term processes that will not deliver results within the life of an average PRSP cycle.

Long-Term, Holistic Development Framework

A long-term development framework has operational meaning only when it is translated into affordable priorities through a disciplined central budget process. Medium-term instruments (such as the PRSP) provide the bridge from the annual budget to the country's long-term framework. Of the six countries studied, only Uganda follows such a process of costing and setting priorities and linking them to a medium-term expenditure framework.

■ Recommendation for recipient countries: *Strengthen the link between medium-term frameworks (such as the PRSP) and budgets.* Donors should support such efforts and make sure their assistance is aligned with national development strategies.

■ Recommendation for all donors: *Provide long-term assistance for capacity strengthening.* This should include sustained support for public sector reforms and institutional development.

Many donor countries are raising the share of aid that they provide as budget and sector program support, and are increasingly signing multi-year assistance agreements in support of national development strategies. However, program aid remains vulnerable to sudden shifts in donor decisionmaking. If recipient countries are expected to adopt a long-term results focus to development planning, so should donors. Delays or non-disbursement of committed funds undermines the integrity of the budget process and reduces the effectiveness of projects and programs.

■ Recommendation for all donors: *Provide predictable and reliable financing* with transparent, multi-year financing indicators, based on clear country performance criteria.

Applying the holistic principle demands attention to the multisectoral determinants of development outcomes—yet most donor agencies and recipient governments do not have internal structures that encourage cross-sectoral dialogue or easy integration of multi-sector interventions. In addition, "silo" thinking and inter-sectoral/departmental competition in donor agencies can exacerbate inter-ministerial competition in client countries.

■ Additional recommendation specifically for the World Bank: A conscious effort is needed to *reform organizational arrangements that discourage cross-sectoral collaboration*, and to develop more effective institutional mechanisms for designing and implementing cross-sectoral programs.

Results Orientation

Aid donors should no longer employ disbursements as their only measure of success; stakeholders should be held accountable for achieving development outcomes. The PRSPs (with their focus on monitoring and evaluating results) and the high visibility of the Millennium Development Goals have contributed to this shift. Sectorwide approaches have helped institutionalize a results focus, and medium-term expenditure frameworks have introduced a results orientation in the budgetary process.

Weak capacity of central and regional public service providers makes this the most difficult principle to implement for all the case study countries. Competing budget priorities, inadequate incentives, and fragile accountability structures are additional constraints. Many recipient countries appear to have adopted a results-oriented approach primarily to satisfy donors. So far, application has often been limited to specific aid-funded projects; a "results culture" has rarely been embedded in the day-to-day operations of government.

■ Recommendation for recipient countries: Strengthen results orientation by increasing political accountability—including citizens' right to demand results and government's ability to respond. Citizens' ability to help monitor results through increased access to government information has been very limited. Governments should undertake three key initiatives:
a) Train and empower public servants to open up information channels and educate the public.
b) Strengthen systems for financial management, performance (value for money) and regulatory audits, and internal and external accountability.
c) Present development strategies (such as the PRSP) in languages and through concepts the broad public will understand; involve the media as a channel for informed dialogue.

Donors have done little to harmonize (that is, standardize) their reporting and results monitoring, continuing to place administrative burdens on recipient governments. And donors continue to overtax existing monitoring structures by proposing complex, special-purpose approaches, with unwieldy indicators that conform more to donors' reporting requirements than to what is needed to manage national service delivery. The result is unsustainable, donor-established enclave monitoring systems.

- Recommendation for all donors: *Strengthen and use country-led M&E systems.* Donors and governments need to view country development outcomes as a joint product, to which donors contribute under country leadership. Results monitoring should be seen as a shared responsibility in which donors and governments use the same information flows for their individual purposes. This requires significant investment in capacity building and harmonization of donor requirements. And it means donors need to downplay some individual interests for more effective joint action.

- Additional recommendation specifically for the World Bank: *Enhance the capacity of the World Bank to continue to track and analyze the implementation of CDF principles and their impacts.*

Country Ownership

Donors and governments increasingly formulate strategy through expanded consultation with key stakeholder groups, in both civil society and the private sector, contributing to country ownership of reforms. However, ownership is too narrowly based when consultations are confined to the executive branch of the government or supplemented only by ad hoc interactions with organizations that donors or government choose. Parliaments, local governments, and civil society and private sector entities have complained of being marginalized in policy discussions. In countries with credible representative institutions, international development organizations should work through them, not sideline them. But for parliaments and governments to exercise

their stewardship and accountability functions, they need better information about the impacts of their decisions on different groups, particularly those who normally have little or no voice.

- Recommendation for all donors: *Work with the government to devise an approach for development consultations with elected officials and nongovernment representatives.* In consultations with interest groups, include the private sector and marginalized civil society organizations. Materials and presentations should be easily understandable to grassroots audiences. Donors should be prepared to provide assistance to strengthen the capacities of these groups to participate in strategy consultations.

- Recommendation for recipient countries: *To enhance country ownership, governments and parliaments should consult among diverse interest groups.* This embraces the full range of civil society and the private sector, including those who lack an organized voice, such as the poorest and women. Several consultative approaches will be required, such as the use of Participatory Poverty Assessments.

Some elements of the PRSP process can inhibit the principle of country ownership. For example, some countries believe that the PRSP requires their development programs to focus too heavily on social expenditures. They believe that because the PRSP must pass through the Boards of the Bank and the International Monetary Fund, their options are limited.

- Additional recommendations specifically for the World Bank: *Clarify the PRSP review process and the Bank's openness to alternative PRSP-consistent development strategies.* Differentiate more clearly the Board's roles in relation to the PRSP and the Country Assistance Strategy.

Country-led Partnership

Country-led partnership is intended to make the recipient country the leading voice in judging the kind and quality of aid it receives. But progress has been highly uneven—across donors, across countries, and across sectors within countries. Effective country leadership of aid partnerships has been difficult to achieve because of the inherent asymmetries in donor-recipient relationships.

Reform will require both donors and recipient countries to make significant changes in their behavior and processes. Many donors face domestic political resistance to harmonizing procedures or reducing the use of international consultants (tied aid still accounts for 50 percent of aid flows). Although donors' field offices have made improvements, the basic parameters for donor behavior are set at headquarters level; it is there that most change must take place.

Country leadership is fostered when donors provide financial resources through mechanisms that apply common pool principles, such as budget support through Poverty Reduction Support Credits and Sectorwide Approaches. But donors cannot accede to country leadership if recipient country administrations display corruption or economic mismanagement. Both donors and recipients need to move faster to align external assistance with country strategies; to promote increased rationalization and selectivity of donor-funded activities; and to harmonize donor procedures and practices. Donor-only coordination exercises may be a first step toward harmonization, but they do not by themselves foster recipient country ownership. The ultimate goal should be to harmonize donor procedures with recipient-country national standards and procedures.

■ Recommendations for all donors:
Step back from micro-managing the aid process at the country level. Instead, provide the capacity building and resources countries need to assume aid management.

Give the recipient country oversight over aid quality. Establish a system of regular country-level review panels composed of independent representatives from the recipient country and donors. Have the panels review donor as well as recipient country performance against a mutually agreed code of conduct and targets. Make results accessible to the public through regular publication and presentation at fora such as Consultative Group meetings.

Decentralize staff and delegate more authority to the field. Select field staff who have proven partnership and relationship-building skills, as well as the requisite subject-area expertise.

Phase out Project Implementation Units (PIUs). Every PIU should be accompanied by a plan for phase-out over the life of the project or program. The distortions created by salary incentives typically associated with PIUs need to be addressed in the context of public service reform.

■ Additional recommendations specifically for the World Bank: The country case studies highlighted some aspects of these recommendations that apply in particular to the Bank.

Continue decentralization and delegation of authority to field offices. The Bank has made considerable progress in decentralization over the last five years. This has involved not only the placement of country directors in the field, but also the fielding of additional headquarters staff and decisionmaking authority.

Select, train, and reward staff—in part—on the basis of their partnership performance. This applies not only to field-based staff, but also to headquarters staff who service country programs (such as sector specialists).

Practice what the Bank preaches regarding harmonization and simplification, program or budget support, and selectivity and "stepping back."

■ Recommendations for recipient countries:

Put responsibility for aid coordination at a high level of government and endow this function with sufficient resources, authority, and political support to lead the aid management process. Strong leadership is needed for a government to consider only aid proposals that are consistent with its national priorities and budget (and reject those that are not).

Implement and enforce procurement and other rules that will engender the confidence of donors. Promulgate procurement and other rules that will meet donors' expectations, and enforce them consistently. This is particularly important where common pool funding and program support is desired.

The Road Ahead

The evaluation suggests several important areas that would benefit from expanded *learning* efforts, including research and exchange of experience:

a) How to establish country-owned monitoring and evaluation systems that bring stakeholders together, building from information and monitoring initiatives in government and among civil society, donors, and the private sector.

b) How to expand involvement in CDF processes by marginalized groups in civil society and the private sector.

c) How to start a debate in donor countries about changing incentives, pooling resources and results, public attitudes to aid, and the role of Audit Offices and Treasuries in compounding the problem.

d) How to expand learning between recipient countries—for example, Uganda's experience with the medium-term expenditure framework and hard budget constraints.

The evaluation concludes that while there is progress toward implementing CDF principles, that progress has been uneven. The greatest gains have occurred in countries that have applied one or more of the principles for a number of years. This finding is not surprising, given that the process of change is still young and that adopting the CDF principles in full requires significant (and often difficult) changes in norms, behaviors, and institutional practices on the part of both donors and recipient countries. Transparency and mutual trust are required of all parties. Continuous political leadership and sustained will on the part of all major development actors are thus needed if today's dysfunctional aid practices are to be transformed under the CDF approach. Some promising opportunities have recently emerged for donors and recipients to move ahead. These include the New Partnership for Africa's Development, the Monterrey Consensus, and the increasing adoption of Millennium Development Goals in PRSPs and other country development frameworks. Another relevant initiative is the joint declaration that emerged from the February 2003 High-Level Forum on Harmonization, particularly the commitment by the parties to utilize the strengthen existing mechanisms to maintain peer pressure on implementing harmonization agreements. The World Bank, in cooperation with other development partners, can and should play a lead role in integrating the CDF principles into all these global initiatives and in identifying additional avenues for progress.

Introduction:
The CDF as a Development Concept

Purpose and Structure of this Report

World Bank President James D. Wolfensohn introduced the Comprehensive Development Framework in early 1999. It brings together, in a unified framework, four principles to improve the effectiveness of development assistance in reducing poverty: a long-term, holistic framework; results orientation; country ownership; and country-led partnership. This report synthesizes the results of a multi-partner effort launched in January 2001 to assess the implementation of the Comprehensive Development Framework (CDF). This first chapter describes the evaluation process and methodology, historical precedents and events leading to the introduction of the CDF, the problems the CDF principles attempted to address, and the relationship between the CDF and Poverty Reduction Strategy Paper (PRSP). Chapter 2 summarizes the evaluation findings and is divided into four sections—one for each principle. Chapter 3 discusses the CDF as a whole and the interaction, complementarities, and tensions among the principles, including how they have played out through PRSPs. The chapter concludes with a summary of the results of a quantitative analysis of the relationships between indirect or proxy indicators of CDF principles and development outcomes in a wide range of countries, as well as the relationships between CDF proxy indicators and indices of the business environment. Chapter 4 draws the main conclusions and presents recommendations for the future.

Objectives of the Evaluation

The objectives of the evaluation were: (1) to assess how the CDF is being implemented on the ground; (2) to identify the factors that have facilitated implementation of CDF principles and those that have hindered it; and (3) to promote learning and capacity development in countries where CDF principles are being implemented. The evaluation was to deal with the relevance, efficacy, and efficiency of the overall development assistance system in selected countries, both on the ground and at the policy level, including linkages to the international development assistance architecture and the Millennium Development Goals (MDGs).

Methodology

Six countries were selected for in-depth case studies: Bolivia, Ghana, Romania, Uganda, and Vietnam—all CDF pilot countries at the time—and Burkina Faso (a non-CDF pilot). Because the main purpose of the evaluation was to look at what had happened on the ground since the CDF was launched, priority was given to interested countries with the longest track record of implementation and highest performance rankings (according to the CDF Secretariat), on grounds that these cases would offer the greatest potential for learning. One non-CDF pilot country was chosen as a control. Because the PRSP is defined as an instrument for implementing the CDF principles in low-income countries, all countries selected (except Romania) were also PRSP countries. Consideration was also given to Regional balance and avoiding overlap with similar evaluative efforts (such as the Strategic Partnership with Africa, or SPA, study of PRSP implementation in eight African countries).

Multi-disciplinary evaluation teams with members from developed and developing countries visited each country and carried out intensive surveys, literature reviews, focus group meetings, structured interviews, and feedback workshops. Surveys of government-donor relations, with a focus on aid transaction costs, were carried out in the five former CDF pilot countries. At the same time, academics and practitioners from the North and the South prepared thematic studies on each of the CDF principles. A pioneering attempt was also made to use quantitative analysis to assess the effects of CDF-like practices in a wide range of countries. A detailed description of methodology and survey instruments used for the six country case studies, four thematic studies, and the econometric study is included in Annexes 5 and 6.

Table 1.1 provides a snapshot socioeconomic profile of the six case study countries. Gross domestic product (GDP) per capita increases sixfold from Burkina Faso to Romania. Vietnam's social indicators, such as illiteracy, life expectancy, and infant mortality, are better than would be expected given its per capita income level. All the countries receive relatively high aid flows per capita, but aid as a percent of national income is sharply lower for the higher-income countries. All the countries have a high level of debt relative to national income; Bolivia, Burkina Faso, Ghana, and Uganda are beneficiaries of the Heavily Indebted Poor Country (HPIC) initiative.

Limitations of the Evaluation

Analysis of the development impact of the CDF initiative is not yet possible because it was introduced only in 1999. Nor is it a straightforward

matter to ascribe development outcomes directly to the advent of the CDF as a whole, since a framework for development processes and aid management is only one among many factors that influence the course of a country's development. But the individual CDF principles have been practiced at various times in a variety of ways in different countries. Thus the evaluation tracks the extent to which CDF or CDF-like principles have been implemented in six different countries and what the effects and implications have been thus far. It reports on evidence already available to chart changes in behaviors, processes, and transaction costs, as well as emerging problems, obstacles, and risks.

Notwithstanding the sound rationale for the selection of case study countries, as in any study relying heavily on country case study evidence, it would have been desirable to have covered a larger sample of countries, had budget and time permitted. Given that only one middle-income country was included in the case study sample (Romania), the evaluation is not strongly evidence-based regarding the application of the CDF principles to these countries. In addition, there was little or no investigation of the applicability of CDF principles in post-conflict and LICUS (Low-Income Countries Under Stress) countries or to global "vertical" programs, such as for HIV/AIDS. Thus, some findings (e.g., general or sector budget support) might not apply to these contexts. The evaluation focuses primarily on the relationship between partner governments and development agency external partners. The CDF principles cover all development relationships, including those among civil society and private sector partners. The evaluation was unable to fully address information, policy, and capacity constraints that keep the poor and other marginalized groups, such as women, from contributing to, and benefiting from, CDF processes. Understanding of these

Table 1.1. Development and Aid Intensity Indicators for the CDF Evaluation Case Study Countries

	Low-income countries	Burkina Faso	Ghana	Uganda	Vietnam	Lower-middle-income countries	Bolivia	Romania
Population (2001: million)	2.5 (billion)	11.6	19.7	22.8	79.5	2.2	8.5 (billion)	22.4
Per capita GDP (constant 1995 US$)	477	250	421	355	356	1,366	944	1,570
Per capita GDP growth rate (2001: annual %)	2	3	2	2	4	3	-1	5
Life expectancy at birth (2000: years)	59	44	57	42	69	69	63	70
Infant mortality rate (2000: per thousand)	76	104	58	83	28	33	57	19
Adult illiteracy rate (2000: % of population 15 and above)	38	75	27	32	7	15	14	2
Population below $1 a day (%)	n.a.	61 (1995)	45 (1999)	n.a.	n.a.	n.a.	14 (1999)	3 (1995)
Aid per capita (2000: US$)	9	30	32	37	22	7	57	19
Aid (2000: % of GNI)	2	15	13	13	5	1	6	1
Aid (2000: % of government expenditure)	n.a.	n.a.	n.a.	77	26	n.a.	24	3 (1999)
External debt (2000: % of GNI)	n.a.	60	138	55	41	n.a.	71	28

n.a. = not available.
Note: GNI = Gross national income.
Source: World Development Indicators and Global Development Finance.

issues and possible lines of action would benefit from further evaluative research.

Each case study used the same set of evaluation questions and employed several instruments to obtain information, including document reviews, individual and group interviews, and questionnaires. A local reference group helped guide the process in each country. Partly owing to reference group inputs, and partly to time and budget constraints, the precise content of the information gathering instruments as well as the coverage of geographic regions and socio-economic groups varied from country to country. Learning and capacity development was one of three objectives of the evaluation. This objective was pursued indirectly through the reference groups and workshops held in each country, as well as through the employment of local researchers on the case study teams and for the surveys of government-donor relations that focused on aid transaction costs.

Background: Evolution of the CDF

In the mid-1990s, concerns were growing about how aid was used and managed, and about the disappointing impact it was having. The concerns were widespread—at the World Bank and other multilateral agencies, and among bilateral aid agencies, nongovernmental organizations (NGOs), and developing country governments. After a decade and a half of structural adjustment, there seemed to be too few positive and sustainable results, especially in Sub-Saharan Africa. Criticisms were mounting, particularly among NGOs, that aid-supported adjustment programs were at best ignoring the poor—and at worst further impoverishing them (see Jolly, Correa, and Stewart 1987).

Others argued that too singular a focus on adjustment and growth neglected the fundamental goal of poverty reduction, broadly defined to include participation, freedom, and empowering the poor and excluded (Sen 1999).[1] It was also becoming clear that the many agencies and international organizations working in developing countries taxed rather than strengthened the capacity of recipient governments. The poor coordination of donors merely added to the challenge of making development effective (van de Walle and Johnson 1996; Lancaster and Wangwe 2000). Some remedial action was clearly needed.

In response, the donor community launched several programs to enhance the effectiveness of development aid: the Heavily Indebted Poor Countries (HIPC) initiative; the International Development Goals, included in the DAC 1996 statement, *Shaping the 21st Century*, and the later UN Millennium Development Goals; and related efforts to improve aid coordination through the Development Partnership Forums in the OECD's Development Assistance Committee and through the UN Development Assistance Framework.

Thinking about a new paradigm for aid and development was also gathering force at the World Bank. In 1998, the Bank formed a Partnerships Group to develop the concept of partnership and how it should be implemented. Ideas for improving the management and impact of aid aimed at poverty reduction began to appear in speeches by President Wolfensohn and senior Bank staff. In Wolfensohn's address to the World Bank Board of Governors at the annual meetings in 1998, he invited countries to pilot a new way of doing business with the Bank and other development agencies, and in January 1999 he proposed the concept formally as the Comprehensive Development Framework (CDF).

The CDF is based on the assumption that all development actors (government, multilaterals and bilaterals, civil society, and private sector) play a part in poverty reduction and equitable, sustainable development. The CDF has four cardinal principles—a *Long-Term, Holistic Development Framework; Results Orientation; Country Ownership;* and *Country-led Partnership*—each of which reflects on past development assistance shortcomings and presents an approach for improvement.

Development strategies should be comprehensive and holistic, and shaped by a long-term vision. Past emphasis on short-term macroeconomic stabilization and balance of payment pressures overwhelmed longer-term structural and social considerations (such as expanding and improving education and health facilities, maintaining infrastructure, and training a new generation of public officials). Development frameworks should no longer focus only on short-term macroeconomic issues but should also embrace social and structural issues in a long-term vision for society.

> After a decade and a half of structural adjustment, there seemed to be too few positive and sustainable results, especially in Sub-Saharan Africa

Development performance should not be measured by inputs and outputs, but assessed by outcomes and impacts, by results on the ground. The traditional emphasis on disbursement levels and project inputs has measured resource allocation and consumption. What really matters is impact on people and their needs.

Development goals and strategies should be "owned" by the country, based on broad citizen participation in shaping them. While donor-driven aid delivered under structural adjustment was sometimes effective, in many cases painful and lengthy adjustment measures were eventually undone. When countries have greater say in shaping reforms, govern-ments and their citizens will be more committed to seeing them through.

Recipient countries should lead aid management and coordination through stakeholder partnerships. Donor-recipient relationships should be actively managed by the recipient country as a partnership and not dominated by donor preferences. Partnerships built on mutual trust and consultation can improve aid coordination and reduce the inefficiencies, asymmetrical power relationships, and tensions of donor-led aid initiatives.

At the heart of the CDF are the assumptions that the content of aid-funded activities is important for poverty reduction and that the way aid is delivered has an important influence on its effectiveness. Governments and international aid organizations needed to collaborate far more effectively if aid were to fully realize its potential in helping reduce poverty in the world. Although largely promoted by the Bank, the CDF was not intended to be a Bank product. It was not explicitly linked to Bank lending, and there was no conditionality attached to it.

None of these individual elements is new; what is unprecedented is that World Bank leadership brought these four principles together in a common, codified framework for poverty reduction and vigorously promoted that framework as an organizing principle to inform its work and to coordinate with other aid agencies and developing country governments.

Putting the CDF in Practice

In 1999, 13 countries volunteered to pilot the CDF approach: Bolivia, Côte d'Ivoire, the

Dominican Republic, Eritrea, Ethiopia, Ghana, Jordan, the Kyrgyz Republic, Morocco, Romania, Uganda, the West Bank and Gaza, and Vietnam.[2] Soon thereafter, many other countries undertook PRSPs. PRSPs were based on CDF principles and were introduced as part of the Bank-Fund terms enabling access to the Enhanced HIPC Initiative. The pilot period closed in September 2000 and was confirmed in January 2001 by the recommendation of the Bank's Board that the CDF be mainstreamed to all countries.

The CDF was somewhat controversial (both inside and outside the Bank) when it was first introduced. There was particular concern that it was an attempt by the World Bank to impose another framework or set of conditionalities on recipient countries and other donors. At the same time, many global initiatives were emerging that were highly compatible with the tenets of the CDF. Eventually most donors and recipients came to support the CDF, particularly as it underscored their own inclinations or policies (see box 1.1).

Several developing countries had already begun to formulate their own national visions for poverty reduction and enhancing the development effectiveness of aid, and for making globalization more sensitive to the requirements of dealing with poverty in their countries. A number of these initiatives pre-date the CDF (for example, national consultations in Bolivia, the Health Sectorwide Approach [SWAp] in Ghana, the Poverty Eradication Action Plan [PEAP] in Uganda). These initiatives emphasize (1) the need for donors to change their behavior and (2) that development is, above all, the product of the visions and actions of the aid-recipient countries and societies. In sum, the CDF quickly became part of development discourse; it reflected emerging thinking and pioneering efforts in some developing countries.

In turn, it has influenced the way in which subsequent global initiatives such as the Millennium Development Goals (MDGs) and the Monterrey Consensus goals have been framed. A Regional example is the New Partnership for Africa's Development (NEPAD), launched in October 2001, which aims to "use joint responsibility, collective action and peer process, and to develop and promote standards, whether of governance, accountability or sound economic management" (Elbadawi and Gelb 2002).

In 1999 the Bank set up a CDF Secretariat as the focal point to promulgate the CDF inside the Bank and globally, provide technical support, monitor progress in implementing CDF principles, and disseminate good practice through workshops, field visits, and regular Learning Group meetings with country directors and the Board. When, in 2001, the Bank's Board decided the CDF principles should guide the Bank's work in all client countries, the Secretariat extended its purview to include all low-income countries, including those that have opted to produce PRSPs, and a wide range of middle-income countries.[3] It has also established monitorable indicators for implementation of the CDF principles, which it tracks and reports periodically.

The CDF Principles

The CDF weaves together four basic principles to pursue the fundamental goal of poverty reduction (working definitions of the CDF principles are presented in Annex 3). Each of the CDF principles is a response to a problem or "system failure" in the delivery of development assistance. A brief discussion of the problems each principle is meant to address is found below.

Box 1.1. The CDF Principles—Antecedents and Support in the Development Community

In his proposal for the **CDF** (January 19, 1999), James Wolfensohn lays out the four CDF principles, giving most attention to the long-term, holistic framework; country ownership; and country-led partnership. The CDF matrix is used to link the holistic framework with country-led partnership. His Annual Meeting speeches contain precursors of the CDF principles. In *The Challenge of Inclusion: Annual Meetings Address* (Hong Kong, September 27, 1997), he insisted that the (recipient) government and people be in the driver's seat and that development "cannot be donor-driven." And in *The Other Crisis: Annual Meetings Address* (Washington, DC, October 6, 1998), he foreshadowed the CDF by calling for a "new development framework" that would involve balance, ownership, and participation. The following selective list briefly annotates several papers, speeches, and events that anticipate or support CDF principles.

- *Shaping the 21st Century: the Contribution of Development Cooperation. 1996* (OECD Development Assistance Committee). Advances several tenets closely related to CDF principles, including partnership, local ownership, and International Development Goals (IDGs—subsequently absorbed into the MDGs).

- *Eliminating World Poverty: A Challenge for the 21st Century: UK White Paper on International Development, 1997*. New policy statement for British bilateral aid set poverty reduction as a goal and proposes partnerships with poorer countries, with other donors and agencies, and with the UK private and voluntary sectors. Commitment made to the IDGs.

- *Partnership for Development: Proposed Actions for the World Bank, 1998*. Prepared by the Partnerships Group at the Bank, this paper laid out the key challenges and actions required to transform the World Bank's partnership culture. The paper anticipated this aspect of the CDF.

- *Towards a New Paradigm for Development Strategies, Policies, and Processes. 1998*. Joseph Stiglitz (Prebisch Lecture, UNCTAD, Geneva). Conceives development strategy as vision for transforming society over 10-to-20 years, with ownership and participation as key ingredients.

- *Making Partnerships Work on the Ground, Stockholm Workshop, 1999,* held in Stockholm in August 1999. Strong statements by the President of Tanzania and the Permanent Secretary of Finance and Planning of Uganda laid out the main requirements for effective country-led partnership.

- *European Commission Policy of Development Cooperation, 2000*. The guiding principles of the policy include country ownership of the development process and increased attention to the social dimension of development. The agreement between the European Union and the African, Caribbean, and Pacific States is fully consistent with these principles.

- *"Partnership 2000"—Denmark's Development Policy and Strategy, 2000*. States that cooperation will be based on partner country strategies, plans and budget; with an emphasis on sector program support and cooperation between central/local governments and the private sector and civil society.

- *NEPAD—New Partnership for Africa's Development, 2001*. NEPAD is supported by African Heads of State committed to a "vision and program of action for the redevelopment of the African continent." It stresses African ownership, initiative, responsibility, and partnership with external partners who accept the NEPAD agenda.

- *The "Monterrey Consensus," 2002*. At the Conference on Financing for Development, commitments were made by developing countries to good governance, by developed countries to increased aid, and by all to poverty reduction and mutual accountability and responsibility for results.

- *Canada Making a Difference in the World: A Policy Statement on Strengthening Aid Effectiveness, 2002*. This new policy statement of the Canadian International Development Agency stresses comprehensive development approaches, local ownership, improved donor coordination with the recipient country in the lead, and a results focus.

- *High Level Forum on Harmonization, 2003*. Rome, February. High-level bilateral, multilateral, and recipient country representatives reviewed progress toward harmonization of donor procedures and practices and agreed on next steps, including a status review in early 2005.

Long-term, Holistic Development Framework

Poverty reduction is a process of economic, social, and political change extending over decades or longer. As a broad goal, it is shared by all aid donors. However, the budgetary and balance-of-payments pressures of the 1980s and beyond tended to overwhelm longer-term considerations, such as expanding basic services, maintaining infrastructure, and training a new generation of public officials. The holistic principle of the CDF was an attempt to rebalance the heavy emphasis of the international financial institutions (IFIs) on macroeconomic stabilization and structural adjustment over the last two decades. While essential for long-term growth, the attention to macroeconomics neglected other critical aspects of development, including the *institutional* (the governmental, legal, and financial systems); the *human* or *social* (the education and health services essential to long-term poverty reduction); and the *physical* (water, sewerage, energy, transportation, and communications infrastructure, environment). Also neglected were the *microeconomic* elements—growth and productivity in agriculture, industry, and services that are keys to long-term poverty reduction.

The long-term holistic principle of the CDF was intended to correct this imbalance. The objective is not to provide a long-term blueprint that is to be followed, as in traditional development planning. It is to inject appropriate considerations of the long term into the business of preparing a practical program with a shorter-term (three-five year) horizon.

The core idea behind the "holistic and comprehensive" aspect of the CDF is that all elements affecting a country's development (and the attendant investment options) should be put on the table, side-by-side, and *given equal chance for consideration*. This is to provide the basis for governments to set priorities and sequence interventions according to national budget constraints and capacity. In short, starting with a comprehensive vision would modernize the planning process, moving away from the "silo" thinking and wish lists approach of the past (where national development plans were simply a collection of unrelated sector plans detached from any real budget process). It would encourage consideration of intersectoral linkages (which, because they cut across the mandates of line ministries, are likely to be missed through normal planning).

> The holistic principle of the CDF was an attempt to rebalance the heavy emphasis... on macroeconomic stabilization and structural adjustment

Sometimes priorities are obvious, as in a macroeconomic crisis. But more commonly, effective priority setting requires informed analysis of alternatives and a political process to adjudicate competing claims. Under the CDF approach, priorities would be set and hard choices would be made against a real budget constraint, and linked to a multi-year expenditure framework. And this would provide all aid donors and recipients with a common vision and structure to shape their strategies, policies, and programs.[4]

Results Orientation

The emphasis on results was born of the concern that development planners focused too much on managing inputs and outputs—to the neglect of outcomes and the real needs and well-being of clients. A results orientation moves the spotlight from activities and outputs to goals. Its practical manifestation is in setting and monitoring targets, to provide policymakers with a tool to measure progress and a framework to structure rewards and budget allocations.

The results focus is in response to experience of the past several decades, when the discourse on foreign aid and development focused on the size of aid flows. Bilateral donors were urged in the Organisation for Economic Cooperation and Development's Development Assistance Committee (OECD DAC) to provide 0.7 percent of their GNP for foreign aid, with aid efforts judged against this standard. For bilateral and multi-lateral agencies, which feared that their budgets would be reduced if they failed to obligate all funds available, rising levels of loans or grants were signs of effective support of development, falling levels as failures of commitment and action. A critical report in the early 1990s described this tendency in the World Bank as "an approval culture" and a problem for aid effectiveness. This problem was not specific to the World Bank or bilateral agencies; disbursement pressures also drove regional development banks, UN agencies, NGOs, foundations, and other development institutions. The new focus on the results of aid-funded activities—rather than the size of aid expenditures—was initially seen as a correction of these tendencies.

This shift toward measurable outcomes was reinforced by several other factors. First, several UN-sponsored world summits in the 1990s produced targets for socioeconomic changes. A number of these targets were combined in the DAC report *Shaping the 21st Century* (OECD DAC 1996), accepted by all DAC members in 1996. In September 2000, the UN adopted these targets, with some additions, as the MDGs, which have since been endorsed by other development organ-izations, including the World Bank. Second, the tools for evaluating the impact of aid improved during the 1990s, with better data sets and more sophisticated approaches to evaluation among major aid agencies. The findings of aid evaluations gave rise to concerns about the impact of aid on development, drawing more attention to the results of aid expenditures. Third, managing for results spread throughout the business and development community in the mid-1990s, including developing country governments. And a number of donor countries adopted "results-based management" systems to assess the performance of many of their activities, including development spending. All of these trends contributed to the prominence of "results" in the CDF.

Despite the widespread acceptance that results and outcomes are important, the approach is not without its critics (see box 1.2). Researchers and practitioners point to a number of ways the approach could backfire if misunderstood or misapplied (Hatry and Yansane 2002). For example, apart from being expensive, a results focus can distort public administration and create perverse incentives. It could, for example, lead to a bureaucratic proliferation of scorecards or a focus on indicators rather than results. At an operational level, managers might pay attention only to indicators that affect their personal advancement. This could create a risk-averse investment climate in which official development assistance (ODA) is used only in areas in which results are easy to achieve and measure quickly, rather than for higher priority investments that are more difficult to implement in a short period.

Country Ownership

Over much of the 50-year history of foreign aid, and particularly since the mid-1980s (the era of structural adjustment), donor governments and international organizations typically decided how aid would be used—designing, implementing, and evaluating the projects and programs they funded. Structural adjustment programs usually conditioned aid on the recipient government changing its policies and/or institutions. Recipient governments, eager for the aid resources, usually agreed to donor conditions without consulting their own people on the projects or reform programs proposed by donors. And while many donor agencies recognized the importance of "ownership" and encouraged participation, in practice they continued to retain most of the decisionmaking authority regarding aid programs and projects.

Sometimes such donor-driven aid can prove effective and sustainable. For example, the numerous currency devaluations in Sub-Saharan Africa—at first strongly resisted by governments there—often turned out to be both effective and sustained by those governments. But in some cases, especially with complex, painful, and time-consuming adjustment measures or complicated projects, this has not been so. More often governments agreed to reforms but did not implement them. Or they implemented reforms and later rolled them back. Or they implemented the projects or programs poorly. A key problem was the lack of commitment to the reforms or projects that governments (and their citizens) felt they had been coerced to adopt, had little say in shaping, or simply did not want.

Box 1.2. Some Reservations about the Results Principle

Although the results principle has gained acceptance in the international development community, it is not universally accepted as best practice. There is a debate over the utility of targets and results-based management. A central concern is that knowing only about outcomes is insufficient; also crucial is understanding the results chain and the sequence of inputs and events needed to achieve the outcome.

Helleiner takes a stronger view, arguing that performance measurement approaches are irrelevant for low-income countries, and that the continuing effort to measure policy change and performance has been driven essentially by the needs of the donor community. He concludes that despite a strong desire to create new forms of aid partnership, nothing essential has changed in the degree of reporting required of aid recipients or the intensity of monitoring their performance by multilateral and bilateral donors (Helleiner 2000).

Others, such as Elliot Berg, argue that that the results focus and the logical framework on which it is based are no longer suitable for today's environment, in which higher priority is being given to institutional change, capacity building, and governance—areas of intervention in which blueprint approaches, indicators, and logframes are unsuitable when compared with more flexible, systems-oriented approaches (Berg 1999). Chapman argues that public service organizations are complex, adaptive systems that respond poorly to top-down centralized approaches, epitomized by results-based management (Chapman 2002).

Advocates provide the counter-arguments that donors have to meet important fiduciary expectations, as do borrowers. They also argue that the pressure for results information stimulates accountability. Even if governments do not like an externally driven results orientation, civil society and parliament tend to support it.

The fundamental intention of the ownership principle is that the country and not donors should be in charge of its development; that identification of development goals and formulation of strategy should be done by the country itself and then supported by donors, and not the other way around. Gaining strong national ownership for development policies means systematic, broad-based stakeholder participation, under government leadership, including civil society, the private sector, local governments, and parliaments. The process and strategies developed are to be implemented with sustained public support from top political leadership and intellectual conviction by key policymakers, and strong links to institutions.

Table 1.2. Coordination Is Needed with Many Actors

Country	Bilateral donors	Multi-lateral donors	Total
Bolivia	17	10	27
Burkina Faso	18	11	29
Ghana	18	11	29
Romania	14	8	22
Uganda	18	11	29
Vietnam	26	5	31

Source: OECD/DAC data; multilateral estimates supplemented by information from case studies.

> The fundamental
> intention of the
> ownership principle
> is that the country and
> not donors should be
> in charge of
> its development

Country-led Partnership

The lack of effective donor coordination has been a long-standing and pervasive dysfunction of the international aid system. There are simply too many uncoordinated actors implementing programs and projects within a given country, leading to a host of inefficiencies and problems for aid recipients. Table 1.2 shows that 20 to 30 aid agencies are active in each of the case study countries.[5] And in some other African countries, more than 30 aid agencies are operating—this is not necessarily a problem except that each agency has its own projects, priorities, administrative requirements, and time horizons, which creates excessive administrative burdens for government.

The degree to which these agencies, often together with hundreds of NGOs, share information, collaborate in the planning and execution of their activities, and engage the recipient government and peoples in these activities varies considerably, but is seldom satisfactory (see Chapter 2 for a discussion of this problem based on evidence from the case studies).

Most developing countries, for example, have no overview of their ODA picture—who is working in which sectors/regions, total aid flows, expenditures. Nor can they predict how much donors will commit or disburse from year to year. Donors themselves seldom know what others are doing, even in the sectors or regions where they are working. This state of affairs saps the energies of overburdened recipient governments and frequently exceeds their capacities. And when recipient governments do not effectively manage their many sources of aid, donors tend to set the aid agenda. The CDF was proposed as a way to address this problem—it would be a framework for sharing information, planning and implementing activities more effectively, and reducing duplication. It would also help recipient governments take a greater lead in shaping and managing their aid—and thus in "owning" it. And the CDF recognizes the important role other development actors—such as civil society, NGOs, and the private sector—play in securing country ownership.

The Relationship Between the CDF and the PRSP

As the CDF was being piloted, a new vehicle—the PRSP—was developed to enhance the implementation of the HIPC initiative. Intended as the government's own medium-term development strategy and expenditure plan, the PRSP would direct resources released through debt reduction toward poverty reduction. At the same time, the PRSPs would embody CDF principles and further their implementation. In short, the PRSP was to be an action plan for the CDF and was to provide governments with the incentives to adopt CDF principles in their development planning and cooperation with donors (see Annex 4[A] for a chronology of events leading to the CDF and PRSP and Annex 4[C] for key principles and instruments of the PRSP).

The PRSP was officially launched in September 1999, barely eight months after the CDF launch. The early guidance, endorsed by Development Committee ministers at the September 1999 Annual Meetings of the World Bank and the IMF, indicated that CDF principles would be embedded in the PRSPs. By October 2002, 20 countries had produced full PRSPs and a further 29 had produced interim PRSPs (I-PRSPs).

There was initially some confusion over the difference between the CDF and the PRSP. The CDF and the PRSP both developed out of simi-lar development thinking during the 1990s, but they emerged from slightly different starting points. The CDF was basically concerned with poverty reduction and the processes of development, while the PRSP was primarily intended to provide a mechanism to link debt relief to poverty reduction. A series of guidelines and statements issued by the World Bank and the IMF over a six-month period following the launch of the PRSP made it clear that the PRSP should apply the principles of the CDF and that the two initiatives should be mutually reinforcing. Through increasing alignment of external assistance to the PRSP, both national and international programs would become subject to the influence of CDF-type principles.

All the early PRSP documentation contained specific references to the CDF and was entirely consistent with its principles. Three key papers set out the approach,[6] stressing the importance of country ownership: broad-based participation: medium- and long-term goals for poverty reduction and appropriate targets and indicators: and integration of macroeconomic, structural, and sectoral policies.[7]

The guidelines for the Joint Staff Assessments of the full PRSP provide further reference to the CDF principles. They stipulate that the PRSP is to be prepared by the government through a country-driven process including broad participation that promotes country ownership of the strategy and its implementation, as well as partnerships among the government, domestic stakeholders, and development partners. The importance of comprehensive diagnosis, a long-term perspective, and results orientation is also highlighted.

Undoubtedly, the continuing influence of the CDF on the PRSP was largely the result of the World Bank President's strong personal commitment to the CDF. His close scrutiny of progress with the CDF pilots throughout this period, his insistence that the PRSP be monitored for compliance with the CDF principles, and his frequent public statements about the importance of the link between the CDF and the PRSP[8] sent a strong message to Bank staff to maintain this link.

Differences Between the CDF and the PRSP

Despite having the same guiding principles, the CDF and PRSPs have important differences. These differences and the tensions they sometimes create in practice are discussed below.

Conditionality and resources

The CDF was not linked to Bank lending, and there was no explicit conditionality attached. It was an approach that governments and other stakeholders could voluntarily implement as they wished (however, some argue that because the CDF was a high profile World Bank initiative, developing countries assumed an implicit link to Bank resources if they adopted the CDF approach). The CDF did not propose a single model or a standard approach (apart from early suggestions to use a CDF matrix as a coordinating tool). Governments were invited to offer their countries for monitoring for a pilot period, and there were no guidelines or timeframes. The operationalization process would depend on local context and priorities.

The PRSP has resources attached to it, but as a country-owned process, it does not incorporate conditions as to its content. It is a new form of social contract with donors for the production of a "credible framework for concessional lending" in return for debt relief, an IMF Poverty Reduction and Growth Facility (PRGF) program and IDA assistance under the Bank's Country Assistance Strategy (CAS) and the Poverty Reduction Support Credit (PRSC).[9] Another aspect of this contract is that as the single framework for government policy, all

donors would align their assistance with the PRSP, thereby reducing transaction costs and the proliferation of donor conditionality.[10]

The attachment of resources to the PRSP has had two consequences for governments: it created pressure to meet the deadlines associated with these resources and a desire to secure a favorable assessment of the document by Fund and Bank staff members. Although these may have been self-imposed pressures, they had the potential to undermine some of the CDF principles. Highly indebted countries have strong incentives to complete the PRSP process as quickly as possible because of the built-in time lags before debt relief can be obtained.[11] The interim PRSP (I-PRSP) was introduced as a device to dilute this time pressure, but international demands for rapid results from the Enhanced HIPC initiative put pressure on Fund and Bank staffs to bring the majority of potentially eligible countries to decision point during 2000.[12] As a result, many I-PRSPs were rushed, and were based on existing policy documents rather than re-thought in a holistic manner and prioritized according to real budget constraints.

Principles and action plans

The CDF is described as a set of principles, processes, or mechanisms, rather than a program for action. It is "an approach," a "way of doing business." But relatively little is said about policy content, mechanisms for implementation, or links to the budget. The CDF argues for a long-term holistic framework and results-based targets but does not specify criteria for them. It promotes participation but does not indicate how this should be organized. It is not, in other words, an action plan. But the PRSP is. As an instrument for policy implementation, it must detail policy priorities, targets and indicators, costings and financing plans, and procedures for monitoring. Mechanisms for incorporating the strategy into government structures and procedures as well as institutionalizing sustainable consultation processes are also required.

Technical standards

The guidelines for preparing Joint Staff Assessments (JSAs) of the PRSP documents suggest criteria of good public policy in relevance, consistency, affordability, consultation, and accountability. They avoid prescribing PRSP content in order to avoid undermining country ownership. However, the detailed action plans of the PRSP take it into technical areas where it is difficult to distinguish generic principles of good public policy from judgments about policy content. There is also ambiguity over whether JSA advice is directed to governments as well as to the Fund and Bank Boards. The tension between ownership and technical standards is never far from the surface in PRSP dialogue, despite internal guidance to minimize it.

The PRSP can be credited for a real shift toward country ownership of policy and planning, with donors relatively disengaged during the preparatory process. But the informal advisory dialogue that accompanies this process in the run up to completion of the document has sometimes been intrusive.[13] The difficulties donors have stepping back from micromanaging country policies was raised by both donor agencies and NGOs in the PRSP comprehensive review.[14]

Timeframes

Despite the exhortation for long-term visions in CDF and PRSP documentation and the existence of long-term sector plans in some countries (such as 10-year health and education strategies in Burkina Faso), many PRSPs have a three-year planning horizon, which broadly corresponds to the Bank-Fund cycles.[15] Some countries have argued for longer timeframes to coincide with their national planning or parliamentary cycles (say, five years). But few countries are fully adopting the longer 10–15 year planning horizon implied by the CDF.

Country-led partnership

The donor-government relationship is a central concern of the CDF, suggesting the need for changes in the interpersonal and institutional behavior of donors. It advocates greater openness, trust, transparency, and flexibility; better information sharing; and more collaborative work. It argues for government leadership of the policymaking process, and of donor coordination and alignment of programs to government policy. The CDF provides both norms for donor behavior and a simple framework for donor coordination (the CDF matrix).

> The CDF provides both norms for donor behavior and a simple framework for donor coordination

The PRSP documentation and guidelines (including for JSAs) say relatively little about government partnership with donors and do not provide a "code" for government-donor relations (though a country may choose to emphasize this aspect—Uganda's PEAP, for example, has a volume devoted to partnerships). The emphasis on "country ownership" has implied donors stepping back while the PRSP is being prepared. Nonetheless, the PRSP provides a concrete basis for partnership that has not existed before.[16] It has given added impetus to the debate about donor coordination and harmonization already promoted by the CDF, by providing detailed objectives, targets, and budgets to which donors are encouraged to align their programs (World Bank 2002a, 2001b).

CHAPTER TWO

Implementing the CDF Principles: The Evidence

The CDF proposes that a country's development framework take a long-term view, that it be *holistic*, that it be *country-owned*, linked to *measurable results*, and that *donor involvement should be a country-led process*. In most cases, this implies a significant change from the status quo. The six country case studies and four thematic papers examined for this evaluation revealed that a variety of processes and instruments have been employed to implement these principles. This chapter looks at whether these processes and instruments in fact led to the design and implementation of development frameworks, partnerships and behaviors that are consistent with the CDF characteristics described above. It also considers whether the characteristics themselves appear to have strengthened the policy reform process and development outcomes.

The answers to these two questions can differ. For example, it is possible that CDF practices will be effective in promoting the proposed changes, but that the changes have proved ineffective in strengthening policy reform and improving development outcomes. It is also possible that the CDF practices are ineffective in promoting the proposed changes, but that where these changes have come about anyway—for reasons other than CDF practices—they have improved policy reform and development outcomes.

This chapter is divided into four sections; we look first to evidence of whether development frameworks in case study countries have incorporated a longer-term holistic perspective. We then turn to assess progress in adopting a results orientation. This is followed by a discussion of country ownership and country-led partnership.

Long-term, Holistic Development Framework

Introducing a Long-term Perspective

The CDF approach, as embodied in the PRSP process, emphasizes that a country's long-term goals should influence the design of its shorter-term development program (3–5 years) and that these shorter programs should be tied to the national budget and consistent with macroeconomic goals. The task of introducing long-term considerations into the rough-and-tumble process of short-term decisionmaking is a difficult one, but the case studies point to some initial successes.

All five PRSP case study countries, four of which were also CDF pilots, had prepared long-term strategies prior to the introduction of the CDF in 1999—preparation of a long-term vision and development framework began in 1995 in Ghana and Uganda, and in 1997 in Bolivia. Burkina Faso began preparing long-term sector plans in the late 1980s that became the building blocks of its PRSP. Vietnam's poverty reduction strategy is embedded in a 10-year socioeconomic development strategy covering the period 2000–2010. Becoming a CDF pilot country gave additional legitimacy and momentum to these efforts, but they were country-driven rather than donor initiatives.

When the PRSPs were introduced, planners did not confine their planning horizon to the three-year frame of the PRSP. Nor has the horizon been artificially set at a uniform five years, as in traditional development planning. To the extent that any horizon is proposed, it is provided by the MDGs, which set a range of objectives for 2015, well beyond the timeframe for practical political decisions, but appropriate for the discussion of structural transformation.

This is important in several respects. Bringing in the long-term perspective can inform and discipline short-term decisionmaking, speed reform, and provide a buffer for (unpopular) short-term policies that need to be adopted. For example, Romania's long-term goal to gain admission to the European Union is concrete, explicit, and broadly internalized, which enables the country's leaders to galvanize society more easily for the substantial changes that it needs to make. And short-term costs of change borne by some groups become more palatable if set in the context of broad-based improvement for many other groups—to a goal widely recognized as desirable.

The repeated articulation of the long-term vision is also important for sustainability, particularly where country leadership changes regularly. The day-to-day political process of policy reform is seldom consensual. Indeed, the role of democratic political oppositions is to offer alternatives to what the government is doing. But if these oppositions reverse plans and reforms significantly when they become governments, the confidence of the public in the consistency of government policy will be eroded. In consequence, the pace of development could slow, and policy uncertainty

Box 2.1. The CDF, PRSPs, and Political Change

There was initial concern among observers that PRSPs and CDF approaches could survive only in states such as Uganda or Vietnam, which have not been subject to frequent changes of leadership. Early evidence from the case studies shows that this is not necessarily the case. Bolivia and Ghana have recently had democratic changes of government. In these cases, the new governments did not completely abandon the PRSP and CDF initiatives begun under previous regimes, though they made changes in name or substance to differentiate these initiatives from programs trademarked by their predecessors. For example, in Ghana, the new government confirmed its commitment to the PRSP and poverty reduction, but chose to change priorities, revising the PRSP document to include more emphasis on accelerating growth. Such freedom to change priorities, essential for the democratic process to be meaningful, indicates that PRSP/CDF processes have not created straitjackets for national policy, but rather can be made to serve a variety of political programs.

increase for the business community. Since no political party can make credible long-term commitments, the CDF advocates having a long-term vision that can help guide strategy through successive short-term political cycles—where rival programs for the short term exist, but within a shared, broad, long-term framework. Under this scenario, new governments would change some policies without systematically undoing the country's longer-term goals and reforms. Box 2.1 illustrates how this process has unfolded in Bolivia and Ghana. However, it is still early, and the Ghana case study argues that in countries with a four-year electoral cycle, the feasibility of a long-term (that is, at least 10-year) vision statement necessitates cross-party agreement and, therefore, a consensus-building political culture and institutions.

For countries not on track to join the EU, the international community is attempting to provide a substitute long-term vision around the attainment of the 2015 MDGs. Although the MDGs have not yet been fully integrated into donors' and recipients' visions, they do have the potential—once translated into country-specific milestones—to put the CDF principle of results orientation into practice. The launch of NEPAD is a somewhat analogous African initiative to bring peer pressure to bear in support of a long-term vision. Ownership of a long-term vision by the Region is used to reinforce commitment at the level of individual member nations.

Introducing a Holistic Approach

Setting priorities is particularly important where public resources and government capacities are limited: not everything can be done, and certainly not all plans can be realized at once. Effective priority setting requires informed analysis of alternatives. The CDF's emphasis on a holistic strategic approach is meant to encourage informed prioritization, more balanced development investments, and the recognition of interconnections between sectors. The evaluation therefore considered the extent to which the case study countries' development plans and strategies were more holistic, sectorally balanced, and prioritized than previous versions.

Evidence from the case studies and the thematic study on long-term holistic planning prepared for this evaluation (Ali and Disch 2002) show that with some exceptions, country development strategies have become more balanced, in that consideration was given to social, economic, and institutional aspects of development. And the poverty emphasis of the PRSPs constitutes a departure from the more exclusive focus on macroeconomic and structural reforms of the last decade.

A medium-term expenditure framework (MTEF) is a critical instrument for implementing longer-term plans; it requires that priorities be costed, linked to the annual national budget, and embedded in a multi-year expenditure framework, consistent with the maintenance of macroeconomic stability. Burkina Faso, Ghana, and Uganda have systems that link development plans to a budget and MTEF. But only in Uganda is that link fully operational and rigorously enforced. This is the most important shortcoming related to implementation of this principle—national plans have little operational meaning if they are not linked to a hard budget constraint and expenditure framework.

> It was often difficult for the PRSP, as a government-led, consensus-based process, to address politically divisive issues

An examination of the PRSP process—as the CDF's main implementation vehicle in low-income countries—showed that it helped open up the process and led to strategies that were more sectorally balanced than in the past (Bolivia, Burkina Faso, Uganda's PEAP, Vietnam).

It was often difficult for the PRSP, as a government-led, consensus-based process, to address politically divisive issues, even when these were direct causes or symptoms of poverty. The PRSPs did not directly address key development issues such as coca, land tenure, social exclusion in Bolivia, water policy in Ghana, and the role of state-owned enterprises in Vietnam. In Bolivia, opposition parties and civil society criticized the PRSP because it did not address "hard poverty" with a strategy to improve rural production and growth. In Ghana, some stakeholders argued that the early drafts of the PRSP were too dominated by the social sectors, while economic growth had been abandoned. When more growth-oriented content was eventually inserted by the new administration, poverty advocates complained that the pendulum had swung too far the other way and the social focus had all but evaporated.

NGOs and civil society groups in several case study countries argued that the poverty policy debate generated through the PRSP was too narrow. In Ghana, several NGOs complained that the government was reluctant to engage with the more radical critics of the mainstream political and economic model. In Burkina Faso, Ghana, and Uganda private sector actors complained that participatory processes associated with the PRSP were unrepresentative because the development NGOs, often very numerous, are overwhelmingly interested in a social agenda, and issues of interest to private sector development were thus underrepresented. Other observers noted that because the contest seemed to be between macroeconomic and social investments, microeconomic policy issues pertinent for enhanced growth (such as improving the investment climate) were overlooked.

Yet, in theory and design, the CDF/PRSP processes should create the opposite effect: insisting that all competing needs and ideas be brought to the table and given equal consideration (and that multiple parties be invited to sit at the table) widens the debate and ensures that previously overlooked issues are considered. As stated by a senior government official of Uganda:

> The CDF liberated us from the excessive focus of the IFIs on macroeconomics and structural adjustment. …What is new and comprehensive about the CDF is that you put all your problems and constraints on the table. You discuss what can be done to overcome those problems and constraints. And then you see to what extent the available resources can allow you to implement the proposed interventions…and you sequence the actions as appropriate given the resource constraints. You say what government can do and what it won't do because others can do it better. And the things that can't be afforded should be forgotten.

Uganda is an example of where the process of prioritization is well established and regularly involves nongovernmental stakeholders. But even in Uganda, segments of the private sector and civil society, particularly in outlying districts, complain that they are not being invited to participate in these processes.[17]

Promoting a Longer-term and Broader View

CDF processes will need to evolve and mature to create space and capacity for debating divisive issues, resolving conflicts, and illuminating cross-sectoral linkages. In some countries (such as Ghana, Uganda, and Vietnam), the CG process has begun to serve this purpose. In the same countries, SWAps have proven effective vehicles for sector debates (health in Ghana, several sector working groups in Uganda, and the Forestry Sector Support Program in Vietnam).

Implementation of results orientation—another CDF principle—can reinforce cross-sectoral interconnections. How does this work? Line ministries are organized not by results but by inputs. Many results, such as better health, require inputs from a wide range of ministries—for example, water and education as well as health care. So, the more that objectives are specified in terms of outcomes and final results, rather than inputs, the more the development framework will need to cut across sectors to identify the variety of inputs needed to achieve a given result. For example, in Uganda, hygiene education is an important component of the water and sanitation strategy, and the Ministries of Education and Health are active participants, along with the Ministry of Lands and Water, in the Water SWAp.

The crucial next step— to link these plans to the discipline of the annual budget and medium-term expenditure framework

In sum, the case study countries have made progress in adopting a long-term planning perspective and have had success in generating development plans from a more comprehensive consideration of options. However, except for Uganda, these countries have yet to take the crucial next step—to link these plans to the discipline of the annual budget and medium-term expenditure framework. Though the PRSP process has helped to broaden the development debate in case study countries, it has not been able to easily address or negotiate contentious (but legitimately contestable) issues that would ideally be resolved through the political trade-offs involved in budget decisionmaking.

Results Orientation

Pre-CDF Efforts

The case studies reveal that a number of countries had begun to adopt a results approach prior to the CDF initiative. This trend is closely linked to the pressure for greater accountability of service providers to the public. One manifestation of this trend is the use of Participatory Poverty Assessments in Uganda. The assessments link the perspectives of poor people to policy formulation, and since the expectations of the poor are framed as outcomes, this has helped shift monitoring and evaluation perspectives. In Ghana, although the basic machinery to foster a results orientation is still weak, the health sector pioneered one of the first and most innovative SWAps in Africa. Performance data are used to review the sector's programs annually and set the workplan for the following year.

As early as 1997, Romania's Ministry of Health and Family decided to move to program-based budgets. Why? It was done to direct national resources into preventive care in addition to curative health programs and to give more weight to funding public health centers in addition to hospitals. Physical output indicators, by program, were added in 2000. Another benchmark involving the early adoption of CDF-like principles is the Conditionality Reformulation Test Exercise, initiated in Burkina Faso in 1997. The test was intended to build a consensus between donors and the government on a common set of performance indicators to be used as a basis for disbursement of financial assistance, preferably in the form of budget support. The government provided all the financial information necessary for donors to understand implementation progress and apply their disbursement criteria, while agreeing to support the government's economic management program and to work on harmonizing their disbursement procedures.

PRSPs to be concrete progress on the part of both donors and governments.

Experience Since the CDF

Despite these early initiatives, implementation of the principle of results orientation has been the most elusive of the four CDF principles, and arguably the most demanding. This is not surprising as there are formidable obstacles on both the donor and recipient country sides, including insufficient investment in monitoring and evaluation, weak technical capacity, inadequate incentives, poor statistical data, and institutional disincentives. Although the results principle has been slower to catch on, there has been notable recent progress: most donors now agree on the need for a focus on results and they are beginning to direct resources to outcome-oriented efforts (box 2.2). Many consider the emphasis on results in

Constraints

The obstacles to institutionalizing the results-oriented approach are significant, and this is manifested in many different ways in case study countries. A number of recipient countries appear to have signed on to the results orientation approach primarily to satisfy donors, and few have embedded the principle into the normal operations of government. There have been some attempts to operationalize the results perspective government-wide, outside the donor domain,[18] but most efforts are still limited primarily to specific aid projects.

A common complaint from informants across case study countries was that donors often propose elaborate and complex monitoring

---

Box 2.2. Results Orientation: Examples of Recent Achievements and Innovations

Uganda's education expenditure tracking study was an extremely effective tool for building government accountability and it is now being replicated widely. The government also publicized results of its comprehensive household survey that quantified improvements in poverty outcomes; public access to these data deepened support for the government's initially controversial pro-poor policies of the early 1990s. The Uganda Participatory Poverty Assessment Program sits within the Ministry of Finance, Planning and Economic Development and provides feedback on absolute and extreme poverty into the budgeting process on a timely basis. Results-oriented disbursements—based on targets—are increasingly applied at the central and local levels. However, these systems still need to be aligned and made fully operational.

Vietnam created its own timetable and indicators for reaching MDGs. These fit better with Vietnam's development strategy, and in some areas are more ambitious than the generic MDGs.

Civil society and the Catholic Church will take an active role in monitoring Bolivia's Poverty Reduction Strategy (which is replete with specific monitorable targets). Indicators will be developed and monitored at the municipal level. Bolivia's Institutional Reform Program requires ministries to sign results agreements (with specific outcomes such as staff reductions) and meet these goals before they can enter the larger reform program.

Ghana's Health SWAp pioneered a results-based approach to performance measurement, and all donors participate with government in the intensive annual review of progress.

approaches, with indicators that are unwieldy, hard to substantiate, and conform more to donors' reporting requirements than to what is needed to help the country manage national service delivery. Most government systems are ill-adapted to take on more demanding monitoring requirements in a short period—and this has led donors to establish enclave M&E systems that exist separately from core government processes, which do not build public sector capacity and are not sustainable. The presence of so many donor-sponsored M&E processes can cause confusion among government partners, especially since donors use different terms for the same concepts, promote contradictory techniques, or push indicators that are internally incoherent. This situation is exacerbated when donors add new targets or monitoring requirements and do not factor in the human and financial costs of collecting additional data.

The Ghana case study cautioned against setting up special-purpose mechanisms solely to track PRSP performance separately from existing systems: "Neither donors nor national actors should focus exclusively or excessively on the GPRS (Ghana's name for the PRSP). By doing so, they risk sidelining or distorting other policy processes and broader institutional capacity development processes." Apart from being unsustainable, such mechanisms promote a "two-class system" of monitoring—one for donor-funded programs and one for the rest of the public sector. Further, PRSPs do not address all of a country's problems, and critical sectors may go unmonitored when scarce resources are devoted to the programs most popular with donors.

Moving the results focus beyond the donor domain is important since the decisions made by mainstream operating agencies (e.g., providing health, education, water, or solid waste management) determine the economic and social well-being of the public. The PRSP process—with sufficient emphasis on MTEFs and monitoring and evaluation—could build up systems to monitor mainstream public programs. But efforts in the case study countries did not extend far enough beyond PRSP sectors and programs to realize that potential.

A recent internal review of a World Bank–financed capacity building project in Africa, for example, concluded that the project was unable to deepen a results-oriented culture across the civil service primarily because the results-oriented management (ROM) methods and techniques were not adequately embedded in routine government processes. It specifically noted that ROM was not initially linked to annual budget and medium-term planning processes, systematic improvements in wages or working conditions, and the strategic review process underpinning ministerial restructuring. Corruption was a serious obstacle in all of the country cases. Respondents believed that civil service reform was required for the results principle to gain serious traction.

How Can Orientation to Results be Strengthened?

High-quality and timely data are critical to effective results monitoring and management. Because macro-level data tend to be unreliable and outdated in developing countries, care should be taken when relying solely on these data to determine budget allocations.[19] Most data collection efforts are now donor funded, raising concerns about how they will be sustained. A balance has to be struck between aiming for comprehensive systems and country capacity. There is a need to settle on acceptable structures that do not require excessive donor assistance nor overtax local capacity. In addition, the right balance has to be struck between central and local monitoring and evaluation

(M&E) functions, because capacity is usually much weaker at the sub-national level.

Much can be done to develop the technical capacity to carry out outcome monitoring by focusing resources on training and on deliberately developing a skilled cadre of M&E staff. In current programs, there are many lost opportunities for M&E capacity building. For example, in many countries data *collection* tends to be done by expert consultants and national staff in the field, providing hands-on training. However, *analysis* of the data is usually done by external consultants back in their home institutions, which deprives national counterparts of the opportunity to absorb more advanced analytical skills, and thereby perpetuates the country's reliance on external consultants for critical analytical functions. Moreover, coordination among entities responsible for collecting, analyzing, reporting, and disseminating results information is weak, and few developing countries have a coherent monitoring system to integrate data collected from different sources.

> Donors need to downplay individual agency interests for more effective joint action

More thought should go to addressing the problems or "unintended consequences" associated with the results-based approach. In this vein Maxwell proposes to negotiate targets locally (apply subsidiarity), use qualitative as well as quantitative indicators, reward genuine value added, adopt the principle of shared responsibility and mutual accountability, and in general follow process rather than blueprint approaches

(Maxwell 2003). Finally, monitoring and reporting is one of the areas where donors have made the least progress in harmonizing practices, and the burdens on government are enormous. To move forward, donors need to downplay individual agency interests for more effective joint action. Results monitoring should be seen as a shared responsibility in which donors and governments each use the same information flows for their individual purposes. In other words, governments and donors need to view country outcomes and the M&E process as a group product, to which donors contribute with the country in the lead.

Country Ownership

Change driven by domestic interest is usually more acceptable and more sustainable than change induced by external sources. That is why the CDF emphasizes country ownership. That is not to say that donors should support whatever a government chooses to do. But when a government initiates improvements in its policies and institutions, donors should be prepared to change their policies and practices to permit and facilitate these improvements. Donors would *permit* such change by leaving more space for domestic initiative than past practices of conditionality afforded. And they would *facilitate* it by encouraging and supporting processes of analysis and discussion that lead to more informed and balanced domestic decisionmaking, complemented by predictable financial support. The most effective change in practices has been the shift from Policy Framework Papers, designed by the IFIs, to PRSPs, designed primarily by governments, with inputs from other domestic stakeholders, a shift that has promoted country ownership.

Countries differ enormously in their degree of governmental and societal ownership of CDF/

PRSP change processes. Since donors require a country to draw up a PRSP as a precondition for debt relief, the process can be seen at one extreme as a further imposition of donor power, and thus be treated in a perfunctory way. At the other extreme, countries can use the space created to genuinely take charge of their own affairs. Ownership is best served when the impetus and development of a PRSP initially comes from the recipient country (Ali and Disch 2002, p. 28; Kanbur, Sandler, and Morrison 1999). Uganda's successful PRSP, issued in 2000, was essentially a rebranding of the Poverty Eradication Action Plan (PEAP), a pre-existing nationally inspired strategy that was first published in 1997, following a two-year process of stakeholder consultations. By contrast, governments have in some instances launched national planning processes almost in parallel with, but distinct from, PRSPs, suggesting in these cases that the PRSP is seen as an exercise for a donor audience. For example, Vietnam originally had two seemingly independent poverty reduction strategies. The "national" Hunger Eradication and Poverty Reduction (HEPR) program targeted disadvantaged households and was being implemented with government resources. The Interim PRSP was an initiative of the World Bank/IMF and emphasized a comprehensive vision. These programs coexisted until the government ultimately produced a Comprehensive Poverty Reduction and Growth Strategy (CPRGS), which serves as Vietnam's PRSP and builds on both the I-PRSP and the HEPR strategy.

The case studies confirm that country ownership of strategy and reforms is more likely to be sustained when, consistent with the CDF country ownership principle, there is regular, broad-based dialogue. Country ownership in this respect has varied in practice among the case study countries. Closest to good practice is Uganda, where the Ministry of Finance,

Planning and Economic Development (MFPED), owing to its mandate to link the planning and budgeting functions, has taken the lead in promoting the strategic investment plans of sector ministries. The main mechanism for linking these functions has been SWAps that are not only required to show clearly what each sector will do to deliver the objectives of the PEAP, but must also prioritize these expenditures to be consistent with the MTEF. The budgeting process has increasingly become open and transparent, following a consultative process wherein stakeholders, including civil society, donors, NGOs, and line ministries are invited to participate in the budget formulation, monitoring, and review process. Increased openness of the budget process has encouraged some donors to integrate their financing with the government's budget system and to commit their planned financings early in the budget cycle. This has allowed government to have greater control over the budget and has increased the efficiency and effectiveness of expenditure allocation. Moreover, MFPED has also curbed the traditional habit of individual donors to exert pressure and tempt line ministries into undertaking projects centered on donor interests. It has limited line ministries' authority to accept donor-funded projects that either fall outside of sector investment plans or fail to directly address priority areas identified by the plans. (See "Country-led Partnership," below, for further discussion.)

The experience of the six case study countries suggests that in the absence of broad-based societal ownership, country ownership is expressed through strong government ownership. For example, in Vietnam the government has a tradition of strong political control, so the CDF approach of letting the government take the lead is widely acknowledged to be "the only way to do business in the country." Where a donor seriously disagrees with the government on a policy—as with the World Bank's assessment of Vietnamese health care policy—the donor steps back. Because it is evident in such a situation that the government rather than the donors will determine the development framework, when the CDF approach is adopted, donors and the IFIs may disengage when they disagree with country policy in a sector. In these circumstances, country-level staff would not be expected to bend normal procedures to accommodate local realities. Noting that direct consultation in Bolivia is "undoubtedly useful as a supplement to the weak representative system, where most of the population does not have an effective voice," the Bolivia case study nevertheless concludes that "country ownership concerns the ability of a country's government to continuously balance the interests of all citizens and cannot be reduced to ad hoc participatory processes. A more nuanced understanding of the ownership principle would place all the country's

political processes at center stage, whether or not they are influenced by international partners."

How Should the CDF Promote Country Ownership? The Role of Participation

The mechanism the CDF uses to encourage country ownership is to give voice to diverse interest groups in a systematic manner. This alone tends to produce a lobby for increased spending rather than a process where tradeoffs are made within budget constraints. The Ghana case study notes that although the Poverty Reduction Strategy was nationally owned and consensual, it may have had a debilitating effect on the making of hard choices. The aspirations expressed by the expenditure lobbies (through CDF/PRSP processes) have to be reconciled with the realities of a consistent medium-term macroeconomic framework, which is ultimately the responsibility of government. While the process of broad consultation can yield benefits for all participants, problems can also emerge. For example, several studies note the danger that CDF participatory processes could generate unrealistic expectations, and the Romania case study noted the potential for participation to degenerate into "gripe sessions." Even the best representations of sectional interests will understate the priority of policies that produce diffused nationwide benefits such as trade liberalization and exchange rate reforms. Such policies are "orphans" in the jungle of interest group lobbying, and so must be espoused by the government itself (see box 2.3).

Development experience shows that a participatory process can be captured by vested interests that use the opportunity to delay widely beneficial reforms. In such cases, the government needs to inform and guide a participatory process, not simply listen. The practices intended to broaden country ownership beyond the government through a wider participation of society in national priority setting have had mixed results. In societies where parliaments do not exist or function ineffectively, the attempt to create ad hoc measures of consultation has had only limited impact.[20] And as observed in several of the case studies (Burkina Faso and Uganda), in countries where parliaments do function, ad hoc procedures risk bypassing and undermining this key representative institution. Where a government is regarded by its citizens as legitimate (normally established by a transparent democratic process), the government has the authority for reform. In such situations, ad hoc, non–government-led participatory measures, inevitably unrepresentative, can be counterproductive. They may appear to question the right of the government to lead a process of change, and they risk undermining sustainable democratic institutions, most notably parliaments. As such, they may run counter to the CDF principle of country ownership (see box 2.4). The Bolivia case study concludes that the various ad hoc consultative mechanisms lack strategic clarity and that there is a consequent "risk that perceived deficiencies in the political system will continue to lead to parallel mechanisms instead of more important changes which would enable the democratic system to function more smoothly."

But even if ad hoc processes were made more representative of sectoral interests, there is an intrinsic problem in processes that bring together representatives of such interests. Much of the necessary reform agenda involves "public good" policies that produce small, individual benefits distributed over many people, perhaps at the cost of losses concentrated on small but well-organized lobbies. No interest group will devote its efforts to promote such reforms, and some stakeholders will try to block them. The proper process for promoting such reforms is for the government to explain the case for them to parliament, whose members, when taken as a whole, do not primarily represent special interests, and who should therefore take a holistic view. Even parliament may not have an adequate understanding of the poor and marginalized. Government can draw on the findings of such sources as Participatory Poverty Assessments (PPAs) in making the case to parliament for programs and policies benefiting the poor. The Ghana case study concludes that "there are possibilities of enhancing national ownership through the further deepening of democratic values, institutions and accountability within the political culture."

Government processes are sometimes seen as "remote from the people." The widespread trend toward decentralization was expected to correct this by increasing local participation. But as

Box 2.4. Perils of Counterproductive Participation

Several country studies noted the dangers of creating processes parallel to existing democratic institutions. In Burkina Faso, the chairman of the National Assembly complained that the Assembly was marginalized from the consultation process for the CSLP (the PRSP for the country), with discussion being limited and rushed. Similarly, in Uganda members of parliament were quite explicit in their criticism of what they regarded as the excessive role of the "development NGOs." Their concerns were that these organizations were insufficiently representative, had little capacity, and lacked accountability. They felt that these agencies were deflecting both the government and the donors from a more direct engagement with parliament, an engagement they would welcome. These observations from the country case studies echo a finding from the tracking surveys of the CDF Secretariat: parliaments have been unduly neglected.

noted in the Ghana case study, and to some degree in all the case studies, the scope for participation through decentralization has probably been exaggerated. Local government structures are often in limbo, still too centralized to connect with genuinely grassroots organizations, but lacking in capacity and oversight. So, without effective leadership by central government, participatory processes tend to produce a "lowest common denominator" consensus, in which complex public good issues, such as exchange rate policy, are crowded out by obvious special interests. For this reason a high degree of societal involvement in the PRSP is unlikely to foster effective change in the absence of government leadership.

Thus there are important caveats for *how* the CDF should promote broader country ownership of the reform process: emphasized here is the strategic choice between strengthening existing representative institutions and building new, ad hoc consultation practices.

How Can Participation Build—Not Undermine—Support for Reform?

Several country studies noted the dangers of creating processes that are parallel to existing democratic institutions. In most countries, however, the existing processes for consultation were quite limited, and the processes required by the PRSP widened the awareness of development policy issues in the society. Even where there was no PRSP, as in Romania, the CDF triggered consultation practices that were new to society and have set an example of how policy formulation can be more inclusive.

While the shift from IFI ownership of the reform process to country ownership has been both considerable and beneficial, the attempt to broaden participation beyond government

within the society was perhaps insufficiently thought through. The case for privileging an ad hoc assortment of social actors differs considerably between countries. Such an undertaking is necessarily biased toward interests that have the cohesion and the skills to make use of the process. A strong reform process is indeed more likely to be sustained if the decisions for reform are seen as legitimate. But the normal process of gaining legitimacy is through parliaments and elections. In countries that have credible representative institutions, evidence from the case studies suggests it is desirable for donors and governments to work through such institutions, as advocated by the CDF country ownership principle, rather than to undermine them with ad hoc approaches.

> The CDF triggered consultation practices that were new to society and have set an example of how policy formulation can be more inclusive

A further potential tension in the emphasis on country ownership noted in some of the country studies is that development programs owned by a developing country government and society may still be subject to endorsement or approval by the Boards of the IFIs. This tension is to a certain degree inevitable. Although country ownership may be necessary for the success of a program, it evidently is not sufficient. Governments and societies may on occasion opt for populist policies that appear alluring but are known from the experience of other countries to run a high risk of failure. While countries have the option to adopt such policies, the donors have the duty to protect scarce aid resources from being wasted, and they cannot be expected to provide financial support in circumstances where either the efficacy of policies is dubious or fiduciary assurances regarding the use of aid are inadequate. However, there is a major difference between the *ex ante* design by IFIs of programs for countries and the *ex post* assessment by IFIs of country-designed programs. The intention of the CDF was to move from the first to the second.

Country-led Partnership

Country-led partnership represents a paradigm shift from donor-led, conditionality-driven, and fragmented aid delivery to a system that puts the recipient in the driver's seat. This approach is intended to ensure better coordination of external assistance, harmonization of practices, better alignment with the country's development strategy, and reductions in the inefficiencies, asymmetrical relationships, and tensions in the donor-led approach. With the recipient country providing leadership based on its *country-owned* development strategy, the new partnership in aid coordination could focus more on development outcomes.

A coherent development program, as intended by the PRSP, is important for effective country-led partnership and aid coordination in low-income countries. Crucial features in changing donor behavior and fostering country-led partnership include ownership of the design of the country development plan (such as Uganda's PEAP), strong government leadership and capacity, and clear institutional and organizational setups and information systems for aid coordination. Where these are missing, donors generally drive the coordination process.

Donor and Recipient Incentives

What are the incentives—and disincentives—for aid partnership? Both donors and recipients must share a common objective and have incentives to pursue it, under the leadership of the recipient, for the country-led partnership principle to work well. Unlike a corporate partnership, where the partners might be driven by a common profit objective, the development partnership is not always driven by the aim to "develop" the recipient country.

Almost every donor cites development or poverty reduction as the major reason for providing aid. But there are other (sometimes dominant) reasons for donors to give aid. Some aid is given for the strategic commercial and political interests of donors. Sometimes new loans are given "to enable the old loans to be paid back" (Easterly 2001, p. 117). For some aid agency staff, power, prestige, and budget size depend on the volume of disbursements they make. Foreign aid also creates and sustains substantial consultancy employment in developed countries. The recipients know that aid has often been given regardless of their behavior. Therefore, it can be difficult to get the actors to behave cooperatively, especially if doing so would threaten their own objectives.

The new country-led partnership principle is supposed to be based on both country selectivity and program selectivity. Improved partnerships are more likely to occur in countries with better governance and institutional structures. And institutionalizing partnerships can strengthen civil society, institutions, and governance structures. Some donors favor proactive, country-led partnerships to create incentives for long-term institutional changes, while others take a wait-and-see approach to adopting budget support and program approaches to aid relationships (Evans 2002). Under the proactive approach, support for capacity building and support for implementation, through budget aid and/or projects utilizing existing structures, go together.

> The new country-led partnership principle is supposed to be based on both country selectivity and program selectivity

The country-led partnership principle is process-intensive and targets long-term institutional development. This is at odds with the short-term pressures on donors to disburse funds, meet reporting requirements and budget cycles, and show the results of their activities. This provides an incentive problem for the long-term institutional orientation of the new partnerships. Finally, with the swing in development thinking favoring social sectors as previously neglected but effective means of poverty reduction, donors overcrowd these sectors. Health, education, and public administration often receive more attention than other sectors and more resources than they can absorb (see Uganda case study). Donors fight for turf, with potential duplication and waste—and sometimes without due consideration for absorptive capacity constraints.

Country-led partnership is also hampered by several other factors affecting recipients (Holmgren and Soludo 2002). These include: insufficient or uncertain political commitment to poverty reduction and sustainable development, limited implementation capacity, and low standards of governance. Donors resort to project rather than program aid because it provides a credible fiduciary environment for channeling aid monies in operating environments often characterized by weak public administrations and corruption. IMF-World Bank studies indicate that most HIPC countries cannot yet track poverty expenditures adequately. Most controls focus on procurement of inputs, disbursement and auditing of funds, and compliance with social and environmental safeguards—all entailing substantial administrative costs.

Changing Partnership Performance: Progress and Issues

Several instruments offer potential to foster more effective country-led partnerships. They are: country-led coordination mechanisms, alignment of donor support with country strategy and programs, more effective modes of aid delivery, and harmonization of donor practices and procedures. The evaluation case studies examined the extent to which each of these is effectively fostering country-led partnership.[21]

Country-led coordination

Progress toward coordination of aid activities by the recipient country is reported in four CDF case study countries—Bolivia, Ghana, Uganda, and Vietnam. Both donors and recipients report that the number and frequency of in-country donor-recipient meetings and coordination activities have risen over the past five years, although the effectiveness and efficiency of increased activities have been mixed.[22] Overall, governments are playing a more active role and local donor coordination has been intensified. For example, the first survey undertaken for the Vietnam case study found that 97 percent of respondents felt that there had been an improvement of relationships between development partners because of the CDF (with 64 percent citing "a lot'" of improvement).

A significant break with past practices has been the change in venue of Consultative Group (CG) meetings from donor to recipient country capitals. This allows increased participation by various branches of government and a wide range of domestic stakeholders (including civil society organizations and private sector associations), and yields more interaction with external partners. CG and mini- or mid-CG meetings are held in Bolivia, Ghana, Uganda, and Vietnam with the participation of all donors as well as domestic nongovernmental stakeholder groups. Donors and government also hold macro, sector, and project-specific coordination activities in each country with varying degrees of frequency and participation. The participation of domestic nongovernmental stakeholder groups in these events tends to be more sporadic. Government and other stakeholders interviewed for the country case studies also report that World Bank operations staff in the field are much more committed than they were five years ago to country leadership of aid coordination processes and to close consultation with other donor representatives. Complaints of inadequate consultation by headquarters teams with other donors persist, however.

In Uganda, the MFPED firmly leads the aid coordination process, acting as the main overseer of donor activities and sector working groups. All donor-funded projects/programs must be cleared by the Aid Liaison Department and an inter-ministerial Development Committee (housed in MFPED), which strictly limit line ministries' authority to accept donor-funded projects and programs that either fall outside of sector investment plans, fail to directly address priority areas identified by sector investment plans, or are not consistent with government's MTEF. The result has been increased alignment of donor country assistance strategies with government development strategy.

Alignment of donor support

The lack of alignment of donor country assistance strategies with country development strategies and priorities is the number one burden that the recipient countries identified in a recent survey (see box 2.5). As of July 2001, only a third of the 46 countries tracked by the CDF Secretariat reported any form of improvement in donor selectivity.[23] Among the case study countries, donor alignment with PRSPs is the closest in Uganda and Vietnam. A review of the PRSP approach undertaken jointly by the IMF and the World Bank in early 2002 concluded that "nearly all donors have agreed in principle to align their programs with

Box 2.5. Main Burdens of Donor Practices in 11 Countries

Recipient country officials surveyed for the OECD DAC Task Force on Donor Practices identified the major burdens listed below imposed by donor practices.

Rank	Type of burden	Frequency of mention
1	Lack of fit with national priorities and systems	11
2	Donor procedures in partner countries	10
3	Inconsistency among donors	7
4	Excessive demands on time (transaction costs)	6
5	Disbursement delays	6
6	Lack of information	4
7	Inconsistency with national systems	3
8	Demands beyond national capacity	2

Source: Amis and Green. 2002 The survey covered officials from central government, line ministries, project implementation units, and relevant civil society organizations in Bangladesh, Bolivia, Cambodia, Egypt, Mozambique, Romania, Senegal, the South Pacific, Tanzania, Uganda, and Vietnam.

PRSPs, but much remains to be done to achieve this objective" (IMF/IDA 2002, p. 20). Admittedly, alignment cannot take place overnight, since projects in a donor portfolio typically last for three to five years. Although the process can take time, this is not an excuse for not beginning. Donor alignment has made most progress at the sectoral level through the use of joint aid instruments (such as budget support through SWAps and PRSCs).

Many of the observed changes in donor behavior in the country cases and other analyses derive from these instruments that implement country-led partnership (Holmgren and Soludo 2002). Surveys show that recipients generally prefer program and budget support over a project approach. This "common pool" or "basket-funding" has been promoted as a way of fostering country-led partnership (Kanbur, Sandler, and Morrison 1999). Common pool initiatives have been under way in Bolivia, Ghana, Uganda, and Vietnam. Proponents of the common pool approach argue that it helps

reduce information and accounting asymmetries in donor-recipient relationships and enhances coordination efficiency. Putting the recipient country in the driver's seat in program selection, design, implementation, and accountability could minimize the problems of bunching in a few fashionable sectors. It could result in greater sensitivity to absorptive capacity issues and improve the collective learning involved in joint rather than disparate activities. In addition, it could significantly lower aid delivery transaction cost burdens as compared with those of multiple projects absorbing the same volume of aid as the common pool.

Despite efforts at coordination, project rather than program aid still dominates, and the harmonization of donor procedures and practices seems to be minimal. Even for Uganda, where country-led partnership seems to have moved furthest along, government data indicate that as recently as 2001 the aid project portfolio was massive and fragmented, with 42 different donors providing assistance through 524 projects and 825 agreements. In Bolivia, despite efforts at coordination, donor assistance remained highly dispersed and fragmented, with 850 projects or programs.

Modes of aid delivery

In all the country studies, donors and governments voiced concern about public sector capacity constraints, especially a weak civil service. And while major institutional reforms relating to public sector management, public finance management, and civil service pay reform have been recognized as necessary and fundamental to bring about significant changes, the pace of reforms has been slow across countries. Consequently, technical assistance (TA) remains a significant mode of aid delivery. However, the customary manner of delivery has contributed to a vicious cycle where topping up of salaries and reliance on project implementation units (PIUs) and highly paid consultants

---

Box 2.6. Disadvantages of Project Implementation Units

- PIU managements are poorly linked to most other government agencies.

- Capacity building within a PIU does not necessarily strengthen the ministry where it is located.

- Selection and composition of technical assistance through PIUs tend to reflect donor rather than government preferences.

- PIU pay scales are typically beyond government scales, causing resentment and distorting incentives.

- Reporting of disbursements is inadequate.

Source: Government of Uganda 2001.

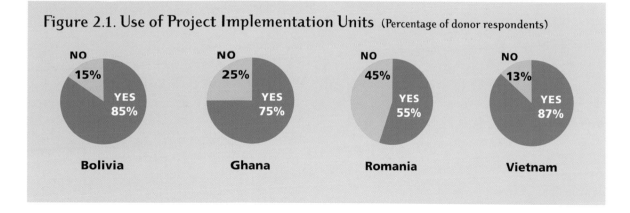

Figure 2.1. Use of Project Implementation Units (Percentage of donor respondents)

have undermined mainline public sector capacity and demoralized low-paid civil servants (box 2.6). Teams in Ghana, Romania, Uganda, and Vietnam heard complaints about supply-driven, high-cost TA of marginal quality.

The use of PIUs and provision of salary incentives for PIU staff is pervasive across all five surveyed countries. The share of donor respondents supporting PIUs ranged from 87 percent in Vietnam to 55 percent in Romania (see figure 2.1). On average, half of the donors now using program/project implementation units plan on continuing their use (all donor respondents in Vietnam plan to continue using PIUs). Only in Uganda are the majority of donor respondents preparing for the eventual phasing out of PIUs, in accordance with government policy.

Donors say they use PIUs to improve implementation effectiveness and efficiency, ease recruitment difficulties, and reduce the workload on thinly spread, poorly qualified field staff.

The provision of salary incentives is particularly widespread in Ghana and Vietnam, where on average half of the responding donors top up salaries and/or provide meeting allowances, per diems, consultancy contracts, and other perquisites to nationals involved in implementation. In all five countries, most donors report

that the practice has either increased or remained the same over the last year. The Romanian country case study finds that salary incentives for staffs of PIUs, typically located in the relevant line ministry, have had a demoralizing impact on regular staff. Donors provide salary incentives for the same reasons they use PIUs. Other reasons include: pressure for fast implementation from donor HQs; common practice among other donors; reluctance by government to tackle the issue; and pressure by the recipient government to have incentives.

A bright spot in aid delivery is the declining reliance on international technical assistance. Almost all donor respondents in Bolivia, Ghana, Romania, and Uganda use less than 20 percent of their annual disbursement on internationally and locally recruited technical assistance, and a majority of these donors report an increase in the share of locally recruited technical assistance over the past five years. This reflects their recognition that local consultants are more in tune with the country conditions and realities, and, in most instances, more cost-effective than international consultants.

The obstacles posed by donor practices
This evaluation has confirmed the OECD DAC survey findings (cited in box 2.5) that donor practices and procedures represent a significant

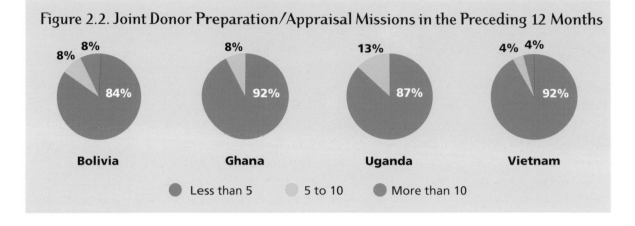

Figure 2.2. Joint Donor Preparation/Appraisal Missions in the Preceding 12 Months

obstacle to country-led partnership. Although many donors point to changes to their administrative rules and procedures, the evidence from the case studies and the survey indicate that improvements are rarely observed in the recipient countries. Three kinds of practices—the number and type of missions, the design of projects, and the harmonization of donor procedures—emerge as areas offering considerable scope for improvement.

a) Donor missions

Large numbers of preparation/appraisal missions from donor headquarters continue to stretch recipient countries' human and time resources, and contribute to high transactions costs in managing aid. In the surveyed countries, donors have not reduced the number of missions they undertake from headquarters over the last five years. In the past twelve months, 90 percent of donor respondents in Romania, 75 percent in Uganda, and 50 percent in Vietnam had undertaken more than five missions, with the Asian Development Bank undertaking as many as 30 missions in Vietnam, the European Bank for Reconstruction and Development (EBRD) between 10 to 20 missions in Romania, and Ireland Aid 12 missions in Uganda. The World Bank undertook more than 10 missions in the past 12 months in each of the three countries.[24]

b) Joint projects and programs

Moves by donors toward jointly funded projects and programs (such as SWAps, basket funding, and cofinancing arrangements) have been limited across countries. In Bolivia, 6 of 13 donors—the Netherlands, Sweden, Switzerland, the United Nations Development Program (UNDP), the United Nations Children's Fund (UNICEF), and the U.K.—responded that over 40 percent of their total annual disbursements over the past two fiscal years was accounted for by jointly funded operations. In contrast, in Vietnam, only one donor of 23 has over 40 percent of its total disbursements accounted for by jointly funded operations. Donors in Bolivia also note that cofinancing does not necessarily imply sound cooperation and that there are qualitative factors that determine government-donor relations.

Most donors report that the number of joint preparation/appraisal missions has either increased or remained the same over the past five years. The World Bank and the U.K. report that at least half of their missions to the case study countries were undertaken jointly with other donors. Nonetheless, very few joint missions are actually undertaken—most countries average fewer than three missions per donor. Furthermore, the joint missions are concentrated in the few sectors where there is either a functioning SWAp or basket funding, and/or cofinancing arrangements (figure 2.2).

A modest positive trend emerges for joint monitoring, supervision, and evaluation missions. About half of donor respondents in Bolivia, Uganda, and Vietnam report an increase in such missions over the past five years.[25] In Ghana, the number of joint monitoring and evaluation missions has remained flat over the past five years, with just over half of donor respondents reporting no change, and two—the Food and Agriculture Organization (FAO) and the Netherlands—reporting declines.[26]

c) Simplification and harmonization of procedures
Donors have put considerable effort into discussions of harmonization of their procedures; box 2.7 reports some of these efforts.

Despite these initiatives, progress in harmonizing procedures is moving very slowly. The number of progress and financial reports required by donors from line ministries continues to impose major burdens on governments. In Bolivia, Ghana, and Romania, for instance, 60 percent of donor respondents require four or more reports per project annually. In Bolivia, half of the donors (Corporación Andina de Fomento, or CAF, Denmark, the Netherlands,

Box 2.7. Recent Harmonization Efforts at the Global and Country Levels

Global Level

The Presidents of the Multilateral Development Banks (MDBs) have been meeting twice a year since the mid-1990s to discuss common issues, including responding to the 1996 MDB Task Force Report, *Saving a Changing World*, which called for greater harmonization of policies and procedures among the MDBs. This led to the creation of joint working groups covering procurement, environmental assessment, financial management, and evaluation. Accomplishments have included agreement on standard bidding documents and standards and good practices for financial management and evaluation. In late 2000, the OECD/DAC Task Force on Donor Practices was established to identify and document changes in donor practices that could reduce burdens on recipient governments and enhance recipient-led aid coordination. In April 2001 the Development Committee of the World Bank and IMF asked that an overall framework be developed, including time-bound action plans for progress in harmonizing operational policies and procedures regarding financial management, procurement, and environmental assessment. The United Nations Development Programme is harmonizing and simplifying operational policies and procedures among UN funds and programs.

Country Level

Several donors are supporting country-led harmonization efforts in selected countries: The World Bank, Asian Development Bank, Japan Bank for International Cooperation, and eight "like-minded" bilateral donors in Vietnam and the Special Partnership for Africa (SPA)—with a focus on budget support—in Ethiopia (with the Bank), Rwanda, and Senegal. Other discussions are being held with Bangladesh, Bolivia, Cambodia, Honduras, Jamaica, Kenya, Kyrgyz Republic, Morocco, Nicaragua, Niger, the Pacific Islands, Papua New Guinea, Tanzania, and Zambia. It is hoped that these country pilots will provide a stimulus to the typically slow progress at the international level. The High-Level Forum on Harmonization in Rome, February 23-25, 2003, provided a challenge for donor and partner country leadership to make meaningful progress.

Box 2.8. Three Donors, Three Sets of Procedures, No Building

A building project in Bolivia shows the high cost of current donor practices. Three major donors in the health sector agreed to cofinance construction of a building. The ministry put up the land, but each donor had its own procedures, which made it difficult to find a common approach to construction. The three donors could not pool their contribution in a common fund, because the rules of the agencies prohibited channeling money to another agency. One donor did not require competitive bidding, but the other two did. None of the agencies could accept the procedures of any of the others, and two of the agencies were unwilling to adopt Bolivian rules.

A "thematic" approach was considered. One donor would finance the design, another the construction works, and the third could contribute the equipment. As an alternative, to avoid one agency blaming another if something went wrong, it was proposed that each donor would finance particular floors, procuring the materials and hiring builders according to its own standards and procedures. This would have greatly prolonged the construction period.

After long debates, one of the donors withdrew from the project, and the other two signed an agreement of their intentions of constructing the building. Thanks to revisions of the regulations and numerous coordination meetings, the donor contributing the smaller amount has accepted the rules of the other donor.

After two years, the foundation stone has yet to be laid.

Source: Bolivia country case study.

Spain, Sweden, and the UNDP) report that the number of reports required has actually increased over the past five years, while most donors in Ghana and Romania report that the trend has remained flat. In both Uganda and Vietnam, where the majority of donors require fewer than four reports yearly, a few responding donors 43 percent in Uganda and 20 percent in Vietnam—are able to report a decrease in the number of reports they require from government. In both countries, and especially in Uganda, this reflects the gradually increasing confidence of donors in the government's commitment and control systems and capacity for financial and expenditure management.

Although there are isolated instances where donors in Bolivia, Ghana, and Uganda have adopted joint reporting formats endorsed or prepared by government, this has largely occurred in sectors where there is either a SWAp or multidonor cofinancing arrangement. In Ghana, all seven donors that report adopting a format endorsed by the government—Danida, the European Commission (EC), the Netherlands, the U.K., the UNDP, the United States, and the World Bank—participate in the health sector SWAp or common basket funding arrangement, while all four donors that have adopted the government's format in Uganda participate in the education and health SWAps. As noted in the Uganda country case study, donors providing budget support on a sectoral or general basis are more prone to accept government procedures, and more so in sectors where joint sector review processes are entrenched. Donors who have not adopted joint government-donor reporting formats tend to be those whose own headquarters' policies and regulations restrict their ability to move to budget support or participate in instruments such as SWAps.[27]

Harmonization has been slow, particularly in the area of procurement rules. The majority of donor respondents in Ghana, Romania, Uganda, and Vietnam report that they have not adopted common donor procurement rules. In Ghana, for instance, only two donors—the Netherlands and the U.K.—have adopted the procurement rules of other donors: both use those of the World Bank. Similar situations are noted in the other countries, where only one or two donors have adopted the procurement rules of other donors. In Vietnam, the Asian Development Bank (ADB) and the World Bank are harmonizing their procedures. For the most part, however, stringent donor headquarters policies and complex and intertwined political and business interests in donor countries have made it difficult for donors to harmonize among themselves. As noted in the Bolivia case study, it appears particularly costly and irrational for member countries of the European Union, which have nine representations in Bolivia, including the EC, not to have coordinated or harmonized their procedures among members more extensively. Box 2.8 graphically illustrates the costs that multiple donor procurement and related procedures can impose.

Monitoring and Evaluating Country-led Partnership Performance: Breaking with the Past

To break with the past and make real advances on the country-led partnership principle requires serious monitoring. This includes ratings and rankings of both the recipients and donors on major elements of the country-led partnership principle so that all partners have the information to continuously refine and improve their practices and policies. All parties must be evaluated, in joint performance reviews co-designed and co-evaluated by both sides of the partnership. A first step would be to harmonize existing criteria among aid agencies and agree on a set of "international best practice"

indicators of effective partnerships. The second step would be to design institutional arrangements or governance structures to mainstream these indicators.

Independent evaluation at the country level, together with possible oversight of donor behavior by national legislatures, might be a powerful means of ensuring donor-recipient transparency and accountability. Currently, Tanzania is experimenting with a form of independent evaluation of aid relationships (box 2.9). These and other worthy experiments deserve further exploration. Respondents in several case study countries suggested the Consultative Group mechanism or SWAp meetings as possible forums for reviewing donor performance (issuing an annual "donor report card," for example). A wide range of potential indicators of country-led partnerships could be quantified and combined in a composite index of effective development partnerships. The impact of the index on outcome variables, such as MDGs, would need further examination.

Conclusions on Country-led Partnership

Is country-led partnership working in practice? The answer is a qualified yes. There is evidence that donor-recipient coordination activities have increased in number and frequency over the past five years. Progress has been highly uneven across donors, across countries, across the various elements or instruments of the country-led partnership principle, and across sectors within countries. Donor headquarters policies, regulations, and incentive structures set boundaries on how much donor field offices can change their behavior. True, there are more joint appraisal missions, more joint reporting formats, and more joint monitoring. But these operations tend to be limited to a few (popular) sectors, particularly the social sectors. Har-

Box 2.9. Independent Donor Performance Monitoring: The Tanzanian Experiment

In Tanzania, efforts have been made to improve the aid relationship since 1995, when an independent assessment, funded by the Danish government in agreement with the Tanzanian government, made a number of concrete recommendations for the government and the donors. Agreement was reached between the government and the Nordic countries on how the aid relationship could be improved, and this led to a broader discussion with the donor community on concrete steps that needed to be taken. At the meeting of the Consultative Group in 1999, it was agreed in principle that an independent process of monitoring of aid relationships should be instituted. This was followed in 2000 by the preparation of the Tanzanian Assistance Strategy (TAS) to govern the ongoing aid relationship between the government and its development partners. At the meeting of the Consultative Group in 2000, it was agreed that implementation of the TAS would include independent monitoring and evaluation of donor performance as well as of Tanzanian performance.

Since then the Economic and Social Research Foundation, an independent Tanzanian NGO, has been appointed to work as an honest broker coordinating the independent monitoring with donor funding coordinated by the UNDP. The Independent Monitoring Group consists of two Tanzanian experts, three experts from donor countries, and one non-Tanzanian African. All members of the group were selected based on their independence from the Tanzanian government and from donor administrations. The work of the group started in early 2002, and its report was presented at the Consultative Group meeting in December 2002. All parties are committed to supporting the work of the group up to the end of 2003, after which the situation is to be reviewed in light of the experience gained.

Source: UNCTAD, 2002; Helleiner 2000.

monizing rules and procedures, particularly for procurement, remains a major problem. Donors still work through separate implementation units in or outside line ministries and provide supply-driven technical assistance.

In addition to conscious efforts by donors and recipients to address the plethora of bureaucratic constraints, more fundamental reforms have to focus on building the infrastructure to institutionalize and sustain aid coordination oriented toward country leadership. Three major elements of this infrastructure include the acceleration of mechanisms that promote common pool funding, demand-driven capacity building, and effective monitoring and evaluation that puts peer pressure on nonconforming partners. Two additional interrelated elements that apply to both sets of partners are transparency and mutual

trust. These considerations surface most explicitly in the Vietnamese case study, where interlocutors said that trust and personal working relationships were key factors in building effective country-led partnership. For donors, this included staff competence, long-term use of "true experts," communication, and dissemination of information (in Vietnamese). For the government, this included staff compensation, information sharing, long-term staff, language, and other skills. A related priority among Vietnam stakeholders is transparency. One interlocutor suggested that the World Bank should add *transparency as a fifth CDF principle*, and argued that the most effective way to enhance ODA effectiveness and reduce corruption is to facilitate the involvement of independent local experts. The Bolivia case study concluded that trust matters not only in the relations between international partners and national stakeholders, but also for relations among international cooperation agencies themselves. Implementing the CDF therefore presupposes ongoing efforts to rebuild trust at every level and among all stakeholders.

Intensified partnerships inevitably place greater demands on the staff and institutional capacities of the recipient countries, requiring heavy investment in domestic capacity and a skillful program to retain capacity. With enhanced capacity, a recipient country is not only better equipped to develop its own PRSP or other long-term development framework. It can also assume the role of a more equal partner, overcoming some of the asymmetries that characterize donor-recipient relationships. Donors can foster the right preconditions for country ownership if they permit the recipient country to determine where and from what source it desires augmented capacity.

CHAPTER THREE

The CDF Principles as a Package: Interaction and Impact

The CDF is more than its four component principles. First and most important, it aims to bring all these principles together in one package or overarching framework, giving them all prominence. It has thus provided all aid donors and recipients with a common structure to shape their strategies, policies, and programs. The potential of this package is most evident in Uganda, and is apparent at the sectoral level in health in Ghana. Second, the CDF, by focusing on poverty reduction, reminds development actors of many of the goals and processes that have long been part of development work—but may have been neglected in recent decades with the crises of stabilization, adjustment, and growth. The CDF is intended to rebalance the approach to development and correct the major flaws in aid management of the recent past. The CDF has had this effect to at least some extent in each of the case study countries. Third, the World Bank's advocacy of CDF principles and processes has increased their visibility and application. Indeed, other UN agencies, as well as bilaterals and multilateral development banks, have affirmed their support for the CDF and the PRSPs.

A sequence among the CDF principles can run in various directions. The Uganda case study, based on that country's experience, suggests that country ownership comes first: followed by the long-term, holistic development framework; then, country-led partnership; and, finally, results orientation. A recent study of ownership of Swedish International Develop-

ment Authority (Sida) projects and programs in three East African countries—Kenya, Tanzania, and Uganda—concludes that transparency and mutual trust must come first, followed by the establishment of country-led partnership. Only then will donors be prepared to *permit* the recipient country to have meaningful ownership and management of the aid process (Anderson and others 2002, p. 4).

Complementarities and Tensions among the CDF Principles

There are important complementarities among the elements of the CDF. The principles are mutually reinforcing and were intended to be implemented together. The country case studies showed that country ownership is necessary for effective country-led partnership, but neither country ownership nor country-led partnership alone is sufficient. A long-term, holistic approach to development is essential for embarking on a broad set of economic, social, and political changes, and a results orientation is needed to mark progress for accountability and improved performance. Case studies also showed that progress on the results principle is linked to the country's level of ownership of its development agenda and the extent of its control over the national monitoring and evaluation function. As shown in Uganda, ownership is essential to the sustainability of the country's

長期

long-term holistic framework, the Poverty Eradication Action Plan (PEAP).

However, there also are tensions among these elements that are frequently obscured. These tensions derive from the development process itself, and represent problems the CDF is intended to solve. The tensions must be acknowledged and managed if they are not to defeat the good intentions of the CDF and PRSP.

One tension is between country ownership and partnership. Country ownership implies a situation in which the balance of decisionmaking is in the hands of governments and other domestic stakeholders receiving external funding. Partnership involves two or more parties working together to achieve desired outcomes. Therefore, greater *partnership* can lead to less *ownership* without the CDF principles. By fostering country-led partnership, the CDF encourages governments to only accept external aid in line with country-owned policies. In addition, it encourages development assistance agencies to align their assistance with country-owned strategies rather than impose conditions developed at donor headquarters. The tension between ownership and partnership stems largely from the asymmetry of power between the recipient country and donors. Because aid donors are accountable to their legislatures or boards, they must require that certain conditions be observed in the use of their funds. Those conditions may not always coincide with the wishes of the governments receiving aid. Despite the rhetoric to the contrary, the recipients are never completely "in the driver's seat." The key in any paradigm of aid management is how much—and under what conditions—do donors cede decisionmaking to recipients on how the aid is used. The CDF attempts to correct an imbalance in this relationship by shifting responsibility to the recipients. This has happened in varying degrees in each of the case

study countries. But in no case has "country-led partnership" eliminated the tension between ownership and partnership. The case studies are replete with examples of long-standing tensions between recipient countries and donors over such issues as health (Vietnam), civil service reform (Ghana), and coca eradication (Bolivia). Where these tensions have been successfully managed, it is because the government has taken the initiative to establish mechanisms and to invite donors to participate (for example, Sector Working Groups in Uganda).

Another tension is between the long-term focus and the emphasis on results. Long term in development can mean decades or more. But political pressures in aid-giving countries often demand indicators of results within a year or two. Despite the MDGs' horizon of 2015, "results management" has come to imply a much shorter time horizon. There can also be tensions in measuring meaningful results, especially in the short term. It is often true that the more quantitative and shorter term the results indicators, the less they have to do with the impact of aid. Short-term indicators do not necessarily reflect causality—a relationship that can be obscured in the eagerness to show positive outcomes. At the same time, to the extent that a results emphasis is at outcome and goal levels, it *supports* the long-term, holistic approach. A focus on health outcomes, for example, requires looking beyond health projects to initiatives in other sectors, such as education and water, and viceversa. For example, water projects in Uganda have a significant health education component. Thus, stakeholders are forced to see inter-sectoral relationships, to "see across sectoral silos."

A third tension involves the possible divergence between the need for a framework for long-term, holistic development and the reality of economic decisionmaking in a democratic, market economy. Although some suggest that the CDF implies a form of indicative planning that is inappropriate for free market economies and democratic discourse, the experiences of the six case study countries show that the planning style of the CDF and PRSP is quite consistent with free markets and broad participation of the population, including in national elections.

A further tension is between ownership and participation. It can be very useful for governments to consult widely with their citizens on development strategies and programs. But this process is time-consuming and costly, and it may not produce clear-cut preferences. Indeed, it could well produce conflict, as different interests demand different approaches. The CDF recognizes that

Table 3.1. Complementarities and Tensions among the CDF Principles

	Holistic, long term	Country ownership	Country-led partnership
Holistic, long term			
Country ownership	*Complementarity* Links strategy with political vision Builds consensus and sustainability		
Country-led partnership	*Complementarity* Holistic – division of labor among partners Long term: wide support of MDGs among partners	*Tension* Country-led partnership implies shared responsibility & accountability	
Results orientation	*Complementarity* Results focus supports long-term, holistic by requiring tracking results in all related sectors *Tension* Hard to measure long-term indicators in short term Holistic approach can lead to goals multiplicity	*Tension* Leads to scrutiny & accountability of government that may be resisted May be offset by broad ownership that includes nongovernment stakeholders	*Complementarity* Results orientation leads to increased accountability, an objective of external partners

in the end, elected governments should be responsible for policymaking and must decide the extent of consultations, weighing the time needed to consult widely and the risk that broad consultations can raise expectations that inevitably will disappoint some groups, as happened among some participants in the CDF Consultations in Romania in 1999. Here again, there is a question of balance—between extensive consultation and action.

These and other potential complementarities and tensions among CDF principles are summarized in table 3.1.

The Role of the PRSP in Implementing the CDF Principles

Implementing a set of development principles requires a plan that translates those principles into action, and institutional processes that enable the actions to be resourced and carried out. The CDF principles alone could not provide these mobilizing elements, but in low-income countries, the PRSP has emerged to play this role. It not only provides a framework for the comprehensive holistic vision, but also an action plan linked to government delivery systems, the budget, and national monitoring processes. On the process side, the PRSP provides specific arenas where the CDF principle of country ownership can play out—in poverty diagnosis, priority setting, and participatory budgeting and monitoring (see box 3.1). While the PRSP still has some way to go to realize all of this potential, it is a considerable advance on the earlier situation.

In all six case study countries, some elements of a CDF approach were already in place before the official launch of the CDF and the PRSP. Most had one or more long-term strategies in place, a degree of country ownership of the strategy, and some experience with participatory approaches. Bolivia, Burkina Faso, Ghana, and Uganda had such strategies at the national or sector levels. Romania and Vietnam had slightly different traditions of long-term central planning and mechanisms for public consultation through official government machinery. The problem was not the lack of long-term visions and plans, but their confusing proliferation.

In most cases, these CDF-type processes were of limited effectiveness. The long-term strategies were seldom comprehensive and holistic; they

> **Box 3.1. Participatory Budgeting and the PRSP**
>
> A review of experiences of one key aspect of participatory PRSP processes, participatory budgeting (PB), has revealed both best practices and pitfalls. By reshaping both the substantive content of public budgets and the process of budget policymaking in developing countries, PB can support poverty reduction, social justice, citizen empowerment, and public learning, as well as build confidence in nascent or precarious public institutions. But participatory processes that emphasize civil society participation while marginalizing the role of legislatures can undermine an institutional counterpoint to executive power. Participatory processes also risk being hijacked by interest groups or local elites, or becoming a venue for distributional conflict. According to the review, realizing the benefits of PB requires that governments, civil society, and legislatures be willing and able to play their part. External actors can best support the phasing in of PB programs by helping all domestic stakeholders to build their capacity to participate effectively.
>
> Source: Bonaglia, de Macedo, and Bussolo 2001 and Heimans 2002.

lacked results-based monitoring, the consultation process was sporadic and narrowly based, and country ownership was limited. Donor support was fragmented and dispersed. Plans and strategies lacked implementation, and had little credibility with government, donors, or the wider public. Elements of the CDF existed, but the CDF was not implemented completely. CDF-type processes were more effective in the context of sectorwide approaches (SWAps), but these were usually limited to particular sectors, such as education and health, where capacity and data were more adequate.[28]

Romania provides an interesting example of a trajectory of a CDF pilot in the absence of a PRSP. The case study indicates that, despite recognition of the benefits of more open, consultative policymaking, the initial enthusiasm for institutionalizing the 1999 "CDF consultations" subsequently waned. There were many reasons for this, including a change of government, ministerial changes, and the preoccupation of political leaders with preparations for accession to the European Union (EU) and NATO. But a common complaint from the 1999 participants was that the CDF consultations had high transaction costs, with few concrete results. A vehicle was needed to translate principles into action. Visions, objectives, and targets were essentially wish lists without priorities for actions and resources: "Romania has enough plans ... we don't need any more strategies. What is needed now are implementation and results" (Romania case study).

In Uganda, the CDF principles were in place well before the CDF and the PRSP were launched and were articulated through an action plan known as the Poverty Eradication Action Plan (PEAP). The PEAP spawned SWAps and the medium-term expenditure framework (MTEF) operationalized the SWAps

into an annual budget (over a three-year rolling period).[29] Thus, a cascade of instruments was put in place in response to adopting new principles. When Uganda became one of the CDF "pilot" countries in 1999, the authorities declared, "The PEAP is the CDF." In addition, when it was necessary to prepare an interim and full PRSP as conditions for receipt of Enhanced HIPC debt relief, a summary of the PEAP became the PRSP.[30] Donor alignment to the PEAP was already evident in increased donor coordination and a rise in budget support. There are many reasons for the relative success of the Ugandan PEAP. These include the focus on implementation and accountability, strong political leadership, and good donor coordination—that is, a CDF-type framework and a PRSP-type action plan.

> Visions, objectives, and targets were essentially wish lists without priorities for actions and resources

Could other mechanisms have fulfilled the role of the PRSP in implementing the CDF principles? The Ghana case study evidence suggests that while *Vision 2020*, the National Strategy for Sustainable Development (NSSD), and other poverty reduction strategies were important forerunners of the PRSP, they also lacked implementation details and a link to resources. The most successful alternatives were the sector-based SWAps, constructed at a more gradual pace, in line with CDF principles, and arguably with more success in changing donor behavior.

Did PRSP Conditionality Distort the Application of CDF Principles?

The case studies report that the HIPC initiative was a major motivation in preparing a PRSP (box 3.2). PRSPs were rushed to meet HIPC schedules, and the participatory process and analytical work were less satisfactory as a result (Bolivia, Ghana).[31] Time pressures may also have undermined the institutionalization of the process, as in Ghana, where a small *ad hoc* group was set up to deliver the product. Even without HIPC, the incentive of the PRGF and IDA financing had the same effect. PRSP activities were rushed to fit in with the schedules of consultative groups or PRGF monitoring (Ghana).

The Joint Staff Assessments (JSAs) reveal some of the areas in which the PRSPs for the case study countries needed strengthening. It is difficult to say how far the "weaknesses" identified in the JSAs resulted from the pressure of the HIPC timetable or other problems, such as capacity or political constraints (box 3.3). Even so, the achievement of the PRSPs in developing a single overarching framework for poverty reduction should not be underestimated, nor should the ownership of the document by government and domestic stakeholders through the participatory process. The virtue of the conditionality link is that the PRSPs were actually completed. They resulted in increased resources for the countries that produced them, and they are now on the path to implementation and revision.

The JSA itself, as an instrument of IFIs, raises issues of partnership and coordination. A representative of a donor based in Bolivia observes that the JSA remains a somewhat exclusive process, involving the government, the IMF, and the World Bank, and leaving the bilateral donors to assess the PRSP on their own. He

Box 3.2. PRSPs and HIPC Conditionality: Evidence from the Case Studies

"There were some initial concerns, voiced on both sides, that in the end, the CPRGS document might serve no other purpose than compliance with a World Bank and IMF requirement. These fears were not borne out, and the CPRGS is fully owned by government and recognized as the guiding framework for almost all ODA." (Vietnam)

"Many still perceive the GPRS as little more than HIPC conditionality or an instrument to convey a new generation of SAPs." (Ghana)

concludes: "The JSA is a good example of an unreformed donor practice continuing in the face of the need for broader coordination and rationalization of different donors' systems."

Limitations of the PRSP

While the PRSP offers an unparalleled opportunity for the implementation of CDF principles, there are major constraints. The first relates to weak capacity in government and civil society, and the second to the discontinuities created by national politics. These two constraints are not specific to the PRSP; they reflect the reality of development and would undermine the application of the CDF principles even in the absence of a PRSP.

Capacity issues

Even for a developed country, it would be a tall order to prepare a PRSP that provides a fully integrated, comprehensive strategy linking priority public actions to a multidimensional poverty analysis and a list of monitorable targets; includes bottom-up costings and relates them to medium-term expenditure ceilings; and does all this on a participatory basis. The requisite capacity involves technical and analytical skills, appropriate information, and an ability to organize, mobilize, and facilitate. It also requires facilitating rules and incentives. Civil society groups require similar skills and institutional competencies. Such capacities are scarce in developing countries and are acquired over time with great difficulty in the face of donor poaching of skilled personnel, the brain drain, and corruption.

It is not just the capacity to deliver a document that is involved here—it is the capacity to implement it on a sustainable basis. This implies

---

Box 3.3. Feedback on the Early PRSPs

The JSA of the Bolivia PRSP recommended an analysis of past policy successes and failures, the sources of growth, and the impact of future reforms on the poor.

The JSA of the Vietnam Interim PRSP contained many positive statements but called for further analysis of policy impacts on the poor, tracking public expenditures, and measures to address the nonmaterial dimensions of poverty, including the position of ethnic minorities.

The JSA of Uganda's PRSP recommended that it pay more attention to gender and develop a special program to alleviate poverty in the north. More analytical work was called for on the implementation of the Land Act, the provision of rural infrastructure, and access to agricultural extension services and rural credit.

The JSA of the first annual PRSP progress report for Burkina Faso recommended updating the macroeconomic framework, developing a global vision on rural development, and strengthening social statistics. The endorsement of future PRSP progress reports will be influenced in part by these recommendations.

---

good institutional delivery mechanisms, an effective budgetary process, and good monitoring and information. In many countries, just as these capacities are beginning to be consolidated in central government, new processes of decentralization will require that these strategies be implemented by local authorities, where capacity is in even shorter supply. These decentralization processes are likely to pose a challenge even for Uganda.

The capacity constraint has varied in the case study countries, being more acute in Burkina Faso, Ghana, and Uganda than in Bolivia, Romania, and Vietnam. Even in the latter countries, however, the different kinds of capacity are unevenly distributed. For the PRSP to succeed, it will need coherent and sustained external support, as well as a lengthy process of learning by doing. The ideal PRSP will not be produced and implemented overnight, with or without conditionality. The process of implementing the CDF principles will strengthen capacity, but this will be a long-term affair, involving widespread public sector reform and institution building. These long-term processes that will not deliver results within the life of an average PRSP cycle.[32]

Politics

The case studies—particularly Bolivia—raise challenging questions about the feasibility of reaching a national consensus around divisive issues such as land tenure, ethnicity, and social and political exclusion.[33] The capacity of governments to implement government policy in an efficient, transparent way is challenged when they are surrounded by a culture of patronage and patrimonialism. A government's margin for maneuvering is limited when there is a high level of public discontent, as there has been from time-to-time in Romania, or when elections are imminent, as in Bolivia and Ghana. This is a clear lesson of the case studies.

The case studies also indicate that despite extensive civic participation, even involving opposition parties and politicized groups such as unions, there is a risk that PRSPs will become identified with the political party in power and be discarded—entirely or partially—when there is a change of government. Thus, even the most holistic, results-oriented PRSP may be unsustainable and its long-term holistic vision unrealistic if only the government in power participates in its preparation.

> There is a risk that PRSPs will become identified with the political party in power

Clearly there is great diversity in the impact of country political processes, and some countries may manage to preserve continuity better than others. In particular, if—consistent with CDF principles—a broad social consensus is built for a long-term vision, the key elements of the vision can transcend political change, as they have in Bolivia, Ghana, and Romania. However, the point here is to recognize that the aspiration of the PRSP to promote more efficient and accountable government is a political—not merely a technocratic—ambition (see box 3.4).

The CDF and the Business Environment

The private sector comprises a crucial stakeholder category for the CDF. It is also the engine for growth and expansion of employment and incomes—essential to poverty reduction—in most countries. Barring such factors as conflict or trade and weather shocks, full involvement of the private sector in CDF processes should encourage a more favorable environment for business activity.

Analysis of the CDF Secretariat tracking ratings of implementation of the CDF principles suggests that despite the relatively better progress in implementing the country ownership principle, one of the key implementation weaknesses has been the failure of governments to provide for adequate consultation with the private sector (see World Bank 2001b). To the extent that failure to involve the private sector in the CDF leads to a less favorable regulatory environment or inadequate service delivery for private sector growth, the development impact of the CDF, as well as its sustainability, may be in jeopardy.

Four indicators of the business environment in 2002 for the 46 countries tracked by the CDF Secretariat and the index of CDF implementation for July 2001 are used to analyze the extent of association between CDF implementation and the business environment (see figures in Annex 5).[34] The analysis makes clear that once country-specific characteristics that are likely to influence the indicators of "business environment" (level of development; whether or not the economy is or was socialist; or whether the country is affected by conflict) are controlled for, there is no relationship between CDF implementation and the four business environment indicators. This result is consistent with the finding that government consultation with the private sector has been less than adequate. It also suggests that there is no evidence that countries with a better record of CDF implementation have managed to create a better business environment for private sector–led growth.

Box 3.4. The Intersection of the PRSP and Domestic Politics

In Ghana: The feasibility of a long-term vision statement necessitates cross-party agreement and, therefore, a consensus-building political culture and institutions. These conditions do not readily apply in Ghana. Democratic traditions are still too new, the influence of clientelist systems of reward remains too strong, the base of educational achievement is still too limited, information flows too poorly, and local-level participation is still very incomplete.

In Vietnam: Planning in Vietnam is part of a political process. Policy content has emerged from long and difficult political debates within the Party. The 10-year and the 5-year Plans are compromises between different views on reform with respect to the place of global integration and the role of the state in the economy. Certain basic differences cannot be bridged by dialogue and partnership initiatives.

In Romania: The CDF was introduced in Romania in a context of negative economic growth, rising poverty and unemployment, and political paralysis. The 1999 CDF consultations gave voice to dissenters both in and out of government. Should raised expectations go unmet, there is a real danger of backlash against the sponsors of such consultations. But the key elements of the long-term vision that emerged from the broadly based consultations survived the change in government.

In Burkina Faso: One of the sequels of Burkina's post-independence history is the heavy presence of the government in all aspects of the country's socioeconomic life. Public debate is still very much subdued, except in a structured context such as the legislative elections. Private media are limited. A high number of rural dwellers confront land tenure insecurity, and their representation at the local level is often questioned. This is a very tough and potentially explosive issue for the government.

In Bolivia: Building shared comprehensive visions—even at the sector or issue level—entails processes with a high political content and potential to arouse fierce dispute. The pressure of deadlines set by international partners naturally influences the nature of participatory processes. Unless harnessed to the pace of other endogenous political processes, there is an additional risk that the country ownership requirement—demanded by international partners themselves—may be an inappropriate intervention in domestic political processes.

Source: Country case studies.

Business Conditions in the Six Case Study Countries

Although each of the six countries in the case study group performed better than average (among a sample of 46 countries) for the four CDF principles, this is not the case in terms of the business environment (table 3.2). For example, in the area of "contract enforcement," three of the six countries (Ghana, Uganda, and Vietnam) scored lower than the median ratings, while Bolivia and Romania scored above average ratings. In terms of "labor regulations," only Ghana and Uganda scored slightly better than the median ratings, while Burkina Faso, Ghana, and Romania scored better than the median performance in the area of "entry regulations." The private sector in Bolivia, and especially in Ghana, appears to face much more serious impediments than the median country in the sample.

Table 3.2. CDF and Business Environment in the Six Case Study Countries

Country	CDF score	Contract enforcement	Credit market	Entry regulations	Labor regulations
Bolivia	3.7	6.0	0	77	3.2
Burkina Faso	3.0		36.4	39	3.2
Ghana	3.9	2.6		126	2.6
Romania	2.7	4.4	3.7	46	3.1
Uganda	3.6	2.6		36	2.8
Vietnam	3.2	3.3	7.9	68	3.7
Sample average of 46 countries	2.4	3.8	13.2	70	3

Source: Doing Business Dataset, The World Bank.

The Development Impact of the CDF and CDF-like Experiences

The limited available evidence on the implementation of CDF development strategies—based on the tracking indicators developed by the World Bank's CDF Secretariat for 46 PRSP and former CDF pilot countries for 2001—suggests that progress on CDF implementation tends to be positively associated with better policy and institutional environments and with successful project implementation (see Chapter 2 and Annex 5 for further evidence on this from the country case studies). This finding of association does not, however, demonstrate causation—that is, whether a CDF approach directly promotes better policies and institutions—much less whether it contributes to ultimate development goals. Until more experience is gained with the CDF approach and adequate historical data are developed, a quantitative *causal* analysis of these questions is not possible.

Though the CDF is new, the principles upon which it is based are not. This suggests that the development impact of the CDF might be gauged by analyzing the experiences of countries that have adopted development strategies that approximate the CDF principles. A pilot effort to use econometric techniques to investigate this question was undertaken as part of the evaluation. The following section summarizes the results (see Annex 5 and Elabadawi and Gelb 2002 for more details). To give empirical content to this concept, indicators of "CDF-like" principles were developed, which are combined with other global development data to analyze the development impact of CDF-like development experiences. The key question to be addressed by the quantitative analysis is whether CDF-like development strategies have actually contributed to better development outcomes, including better institutions, higher growth, lower poverty, and enhanced human development, as well as greater aid effectiveness.

CDF-like Indices

For each of the CDF principles an index was constructed as follows:

- *Long-term, Holistic Development Framework.* An index of the dispersion in ratings of policy and institutional quality across three broad sectors is viewed as a measure of a country's ability to maintain balanced development, an expected outcome of implementation of the long-term, holistic principle.[35] A large dispersion among the three sectors suggests failure to adopt a long-term, holistic approach to development.

■ *Results Orientation.* An index of the quality of poverty monitoring.[36]

■ *Country Ownership.* A simple average of four components of a widely quoted index on democracy (the "Polity IV index"), including governance indicators that account for participation and accountability.

■ *Country-led Partnership.* An index composed of two elements that seek to measure the quality of aid delivery: first, the concentration of donors in the country as a whole divided by the sectoral concentration of aid; and, second, an index of "excessive" technical assistance, which is measured by the ratio of optimum to actual technical assistance (see Annex 5 for further details).[37]

The overall CDF-like index is a simple average of the four indicators of CDF-like principles, which regards all principles as equally important for shaping a CDF development strategy. The indicators are constructed for 88 countries

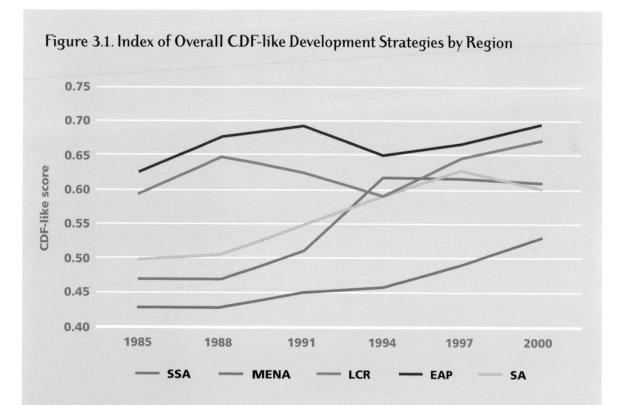

Figure 3.1. Index of Overall CDF-like Development Strategies by Region

Note: Of the 88 countries, 36 are classified as low-income countries, 33 as low-middle-income, and 19 as higher income: Sub-Saharan Africa (SSA, 26 countries); Middle East and North Africa (MENA, 7 countries); Latin America and Caribbean (LCR, 23 countries); East Asia and Pacific (EAP, 7 countries); South Asia (SA, 5 countries).

East European countries are not included in the figure because the indexes are only available for the 1990s. See Annex 5 for explicit algebraic expressions of the indicators of CDF-like principles and a complete list of countries. The CDF-like index and the four component indicators are normalized to fall between 0.0 and 1.0.

(including the 46 countries tracked by the CDF Secretariat) for 1980-2000.

Figure 3.1 suggests that the CDF-like index roughly tracks with development experiences pursued over the last 20 years or so. It suggests that the development experiences in East Asia have tended to approximate CDF strategies more closely than have the experiences of other regional comparators, and that Sub-Saharan Africa has substantially failed to approximate the CDF vision of development, despite having improved quite sharply since 1994.

The Determinants of CDF-like Development Strategies

A country's propensity to adopt a CDF-like development strategy, as well as good policy and institutional environment, may be driven by fundamental factors such as initial level of development, the degree of social cohesion,

and the capacity of society to mediate conflict among different economic or social groups, in addition to exogenous factors. The evidence strongly supports the hypothesis that: *The choice of CDF-like development strategies is endogenous to such structural and social factors*. Countries with initial conditions of a higher level of development (higher per capita income), high social cohesion (lower ethnic fractionalization) (Rodrick 1999),[38] and better institutions for promoting cooperation among social groups (functioning democratic and civil society institutions) tend to adopt CDF-like development strategies. Moreover, with functioning democratic institutions, even highly fractionalized societies could manage to achieve a CDF-like development approach. Figure 3.2 shows how much these structural and social factors are associated with the index of CDF-like strategies. The same findings also apply to the overall institutional and policy environment as

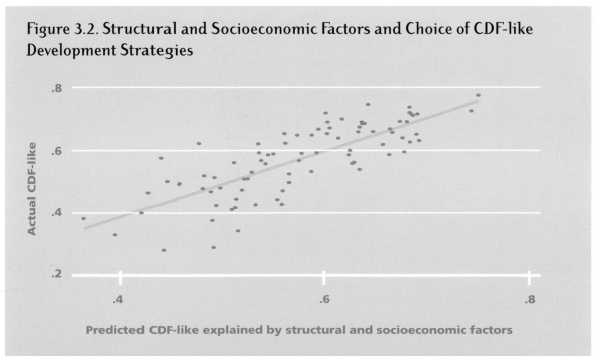

Figure 3.2. Structural and Socioeconomic Factors and Choice of CDF-like Development Strategies

Predicted CDF-like explained by structural and socioeconomic factors

Note: Based on the regression equation of column (2) of table 4, Elbadawi, Mavrotas, and Randa 2003. Independent variables used are initial per capita income, social fractionalization, democracy and the interaction between democracy and social fractionalization.

measured by the Country Policy and Institutional Assessment (CPIA) (see Elbadawi, Mavrotas, and Randa 2003, table 4).[39] The same analysis also finds that the fundamental economic and social factors do not influence institutions and policy (the CPIA) once the CDF-like index has been taken into account.[40] This suggests that these fundamental factors shape policies and institutions through the development processes and strategies measured by the CDF-like indices.

Sustaining CDF-like development is more challenging in fractionalized societies. The literature suggests that societies with socially or economically divided societies and weak institutions for mediating conflicts among group interests are more likely to experience policy reversals and thus be unable to sustain growth (see Rodrik 1999 and Elbadawi 2001). In CDF implementation, it has also been noted that sustainability becomes a problem when countries are facing economic crisis. In such countries, macroeconomic issues dominate social and structural ones in terms of policy priorities (World Bank 2001a, p. 8). The analysis here confirms this observation. The volatility of the overall CDF-like strategy indicator is positively associated with terms of trade shocks, social fractionalization, and autocracy (see table 4 of Elbadawi, Mavrotas, and Randa 2003).

Impact on Institutions, Growth, and Literacy

A country's decision to adopt a CDF-like (or any other type of) development strategy is endogenous to country-specific socioeconomic and political characteristics. These same factors are also likely to be important determinants of country economic performance. The marginal contribution of a CDF-like strategy to growth, institutions, and literacy is estimated by employing a model that accounts for the above complications (see table 5 of Elbadawi, Mavrotas, and Randa 2003), and corrects for the bias that

Table 3.3. Marginal Contribution of CDF-like Development

(Percent change in dependent variable associated with a 1% increase in the "Overall CDF-like Index")

Dependent variable	Marginal contribution of overall CDF-like index (in elasticity form)
GDP growth	2.68
Institutions (CPIA as a proxy indicator)	0.57
Adult illiteracy	-0.89

Note: The table contains the derived long-run elasticities based on coefficients of the "predicted" overall CDF-like index from the regressions of table 5 of Elbadawi, Mavrotas, and Randa 2003 in the performance equation for growth, CPIA, and illiteracy. The mean of the predicted CDF = 0.58, growth = 3.73, CPIA = 3.14, illiteracy rate = 32.24 [Top quartile of CDF = 0.66].

results from the non-randomness of the decision to pursue a CDF-like development strategy.

CDF-like development strategies produce superior development outcomes. The magnitudes of these marginal impacts can be translated into elasticity estimates (table 3.3). These estimates suggest that moving up the ladder to a more comprehensive CDF-like development strategy could have substantial development impact. While these results are only suggestive, they do imply that the development impact of CDF-like development strategies is not negligible. Take the case of Africa, which constitutes the most serious challenge for development. A recent study finds that in a sample of 44 African countries, 8 had negative growth rates in 2000 and 14 had growth rates of less than 3 percent (Elbadawi and Gelb 2002). Only 7 countries currently have growth rates high enough to prevent poverty from rising by 2015. For the remaining 37 countries, poverty is expected to *increase* rather than decrease under prevailing growth rates. The results of this analysis suggest that if the 22 African countries with an average rate of growth of 1.5 percent were to improve their CDF-like development index by a third, to reach the median for South Asia (from 40 to 60), their growth rates would approach the 5 percent threshold needed to prevent poverty from rising.

> These results ...imply that the development impact of CDF-like development strategies is not negligible

Aid Effectiveness of CDF Development Strategies

Having identified a likely positive development impact of CDF-like development strategies, it is natural to subsequently investigate whether these strategies make aid more effective—or, put differently, whether there are higher payoffs to be gained by providing aid to countries pursuing CDF-like development strategies. This analysis is based on estimation of an extended growth model, which in addition to accounting for policy environment also controls for the type of development strategy, as measured by the CDF-like index (table 7, Elbadawi, Mavrotas, and Randa 2003).

■ *CDF-like development strategies enhance aid effectiveness.* Simulation analysis based on the above models suggests that there could be high payoffs from providing aid to countries pursuing CDF-like development strate-

gies. For example, a 10 percentage point increase in the CDF-like index would accelerate growth by 9 percent for any given level of aid.

Conclusions and Some Policy Implications

The following conclusions emerge from the econometric analysis. *First,* CDF-like development strategies, as well as institutions, are endogenous to "deep" country-specific characteristics, such as initial level of economic and political development and extent of social fractionalization. *Second,* these country characteristics appear to influence institutions through the processes associated with CDF-like development strategies. *Third,* sustaining a CDF-like development strategy is more challenging in fractionalized societies with weak institutions for promoting inter–social group cooperation, especially when faced with external shocks. This finding has two important implications for the design of future CDF implementation. More attention should be given to flexible and counter-cyclical assistance programs to help aid-recipient and other middle-income countries smooth the impact of external shocks. At a deeper level, the PRSP and other lending instruments should provide more time and space for a genuine national bargaining process to evolve and mature, especially in fractionalized societies. *Fourth,* CDF-like development strategies appear to produce superior development outcomes. Analysis of growth, poverty reduction, and human development indicators seem to suggest that a CDF-like development strategy has made positive marginal contributions to these pivotal development indicators. *Finally,* a CDF-like development strategy increases aid-effectiveness, where simulations based on analysis of growth suggest that there could be very high payoffs to be gained by providing aid to countries pursuing CDF-like development strategies.

CHAPTER FOUR

Conclusions and Recommendations

The CDF principles are individually and collectively important. A major value added of the CDF initiative has been to bring all the individual principles together as a package and promulgate them on the global agenda, initially through the personal advocacy of the World Bank's President, and more recently through the PRSP mechanism.

While the CDF alone is not sufficient for poverty reduction, it does comprise fundamental and necessary principles for strategic development planning and key development cooperation processes, without which sustained poverty reduction would be unlikely to occur. The process of change is young and the full benefits of the CDF approach are unlikely to be realized quickly, painlessly, or without cost. It is clear that all parties will need to make changes if current inefficient aid practices are to be rationalized and the ambitious development targets set out in the MDGs and the international consensus that emerged from the Monterrey Conference are to be met.

The evaluation also found that there can be tensions in how the CDF principles are applied, specifically involving ownership and partnership, and the long-term focus and the emphasis on results. These tensions have been longstanding in development practice and are neither novel nor unique to the CDF. There is also evidence at the country level that the CDF principles can be complementary. Country leadership, whether at the highest levels of government, in line ministries, or among elected officials, remains a critical factor for making and sustaining progress on each of the principles and for managing CDF processes so they are complementary—e.g., country ownership and country-led partnership processes. In the case study countries, government leadership appears fundamental to sustaining the long-term vision; fostering adequate processes for broad country ownership of that vision; managing development cooperation at the country level; and enhancing the profile of monitoring and evaluation findings by using them in decisionmaking. A lack of leadership in any of these areas poses a key obstacle. The case studies also show that donors can play an important enabling role by supporting enhanced country leadership on various levels through capacity building, the use of more flexible financing arrangements, and the simplification and harmonization of processes.

This chapter draws the evaluation's main conclusions about the implementation of the CDF principles, and makes recommendations for the consideration of donors and recipient countries. Recommendations for donors apply to all donors, international financial institutions, and bilateral and multilateral development agencies. The recommendations for donors include several specifically directed to the World Bank as the initiator of the CDF and lead sponsor of the CDF evaluation.

Long-term, Holistic Framework

Conclusions: Long-term development frameworks have operational meaning only if they are translated into affordable priorities through a disciplined budget process. Development strategies without a hard budget constraint are merely "wish lists." Without a link to an annual budget process, there is no guarantee that resources will not be diverted away from priorities identified in the PRSP process to other ministry or donor interests. A development framework linked to the budget is thus necessary as (i) a rationale for the allocation of resources; (ii) a basis for country-led partnerships; and (iii) a framework for assessing results. At the same time, the PRSP and other similar medium-term instruments need to be anchored in a longer-term framework if they are to achieve long-range goals.

Five of the six case study countries now have PRSPs that call for linking development frameworks to the budget process. While several countries, including Burkina Faso and Ghana, have adopted medium-term expenditure frameworks (MTEFs), few follow as rigorous a process as Uganda in costing and setting priorities, and grounding the PRSP in the short-term budget process through the MTEF. In Ghana, for example, the MTEF exists on paper, but has yet to exert influence on everyday fiscal realities.

The PRSP is a powerful tool for implementing the CDF principles, and from the perspective of advancing CDF-like principles, it merits continued support and development. For middle-income countries and others not following the PRSP track, different instruments and mechanisms will be required, but have not yet clearly emerged.[41] For the PRSP to succeed, it will need coherent and sustained external support, as well as a lengthy process of learning by doing. The public sector reform and institution building that the PRSP requires for success are long-term processes that will not deliver results within the life of a single PRSP cycle.

> Development strategies without a hard budget constraint are merely "wish lists"

Recommendation for recipient countries: *Strengthen the link between long-term frameworks and budgets*. Strengthening the link between longer-term plans, such as the PRSP, and the budget or MTEF should be a priority if countries are to maximize the operational usefulness of the national development plan for making policy choices in the context of limited resources. Donors should support such efforts.

Recommendation for all donors: *Provide-long-term assistance for capacity strengthening*. This should include sustained support for public sector reforms and institutional development.

Conclusions: If recipient countries are expected to adopt a long-term approach for solving development problems, so too should donors. It is encouraging that many donor countries are now increasing the share of budget and sector program support, signing more long-term indicative funding agreements, and basing their assistance on the recipient's own long-term development strategy and MTEF. Yet recipient governments and some donors express concern that program aid is still vulnerable to sudden shifts in donor decisionmaking. Recipient countries in particular argue that it is difficult to plan when aid flows are not predictable beyond annual commitments, and disbursements are not timely or reliable.

Recommendation for all donors: *Provide predictable and reliable financing.* Donors need to provide predictable, transparent, and multi-year indicators of financing, based on clear, mutually agreed country performance criteria. They should ensure that disbursement is not interrupted unexpectedly. The PRSP provides an organizing framework for multi-year commitments.

Additional recommendation specifically for the World Bank: *Improve cross-sectoral programming and implementation.* The Bank's internal structure, which organizes staff mainly by sectoral specialties, can sometimes discourage cross-sectoral dialogue and integration of interventions. This can exacerbate "silo" thinking or inter-ministerial competition in client countries. Efforts that are cross-sectoral by nature, such as gender or decentralization, also face these challenges. Conscious effort is needed to counteract the sectoral focus of organizational arrangements and to support a holistic program that links vision, budgets, and results.

Results Orientation

Conclusions: Progress in implementing the *results orientation* principle has been the most elusive of the four CDF principles. There are a number of reasons for this: weak technical capacity, poor statistical data, inadequate incentives, inappropriate analytical tools, and lack of demand for monitoring and evaluation results. Furthermore, efforts to ensure policy change and performance have been driven primarily by needs of the donor community, and the desire for new forms of aid partnership have not yet led to significant change in the degree or type of aid reporting required (see box 1.2). Finally, results orientation requires countries to have strong capacity not only in monitoring but also in budgeting, execution of budgets, and financial and political accountability.

There has been some progress on this principle, despite the many constraints. The discourse has shifted from aid expenditures as a measure of achievement to increasing acceptance that stakeholders should be held accountable for achieving development outcomes. The PRSPs and the high visibility of the MDGs have contributed to this shift. SWAps have helped to institutionalize a results focus and MTEFs have emerged as a viable vehicle for introducing a results orientation into the budgetary process. Still, many recipient countries appear to have adopted a results-oriented approach primarily to satisfy donors, at least initially. Application of the results approach is primarily limited to specific aid-funded projects and has rarely been embedded in the normal operations of government. And donors continue to encourage the development of measurement systems that meet their own institutional needs first and foremost.

Recommendations for recipient countries: *Results orientation through greater accountability to the public.* Worthwhile as specific monitoring mechanisms may be for learning and for accountability to donors, the key to a greater results orientation is strengthening the political accountability of the government to citizens. But citizens' channels to demand results and participate in development policy debates have been very limited. The country case studies (and lessons from innovation in other countries) suggest several measures governments can undertake to strengthen public accountability:

1) Train and expect public servants to open up policy and program information channels, and educate the public to participate.

2) Strengthen systems for financial management, performance ("value for money"), and regulatory audits, and internal and external accountability.

3) Provide development plans in languages and through concepts the broad public will understand; use the media to support informed dialogue and demand for results.

4) Engage civil society organizations in budget and implementation monitoring and employ participatory poverty assessments (PPAs) and other monitoring approaches in order to obtain feedback from the poor and marginalized on policies that impact them.

5) Develop and use instruments such as "citizen service delivery report cards," used in Ghana and proposed in Vietnam, among other countries, or the recently passed Freedom of Information Act in Romania.

Conclusions: Donors continue to overtax existing monitoring structures by proposing complex, special-purpose approaches, with indicators that are unwieldy, difficult to substantiate, and conform more to donors' reporting requirements than to the needs of service delivery management. This is exacerbated by the proliferation of project implementation units (PIUs) for project management purposes. Donor-established enclave monitoring systems are not sustainable, and can even weaken local capacity.

Recommendation for all donors: *Strengthen and utilize country-led M&E systems.* Donors should downplay individual interests in favor of effective joint action in strengthening and utilizing country monitoring and evaluation systems. Real progress will be realized only when governments and donors view country development outcomes as a joint product, to which donors contribute with the country in the lead. It will also require significant investment in capacity building. While there are great systemic gains to be had from making these changes, there are currently few tangible incentives—individual or agency—to motivate that change. Donors need

to educate their own constituencies (politicians, audit offices, treasury, and the public) about the limited value of trying to attribute increasingly complex development outcomes to single-agency interventions.

Donors should invest in further exploration and exchange on the following: (a) how to establish country-owned M&E systems that bring stakeholders together and that build from PPAs, budget monitoring processes, and other recent innovations; (b) how to include M&E of donor performance; and (c) how to start a debate in donor countries about changing incentives; pooling resources and results; and attitudes about aid, accountability, and donor attribution.

Additional recommendation specifically for the World Bank: *Enhance the capacity of the World Bank to track and analyze the implementation of CDF principles and their impacts.* The tracking activity undertaken by the CDF Secretariat of the World Bank provides one mechanism for periodic assessment of CDF processes. To permit rigorous causal analysis of the impact of the CDF on development and intermediate goals, the generation of quantifiable tracking indicators on a regular and systematic basis should be a top priority. The CDF Secretariat should also work toward acquiring the necessary quantitative and analytical skills to undertake impact analysis on a regular basis. This analysis should take into account the views of other stakeholders (donors as well as recipient country governments and other key groups) about the evolution, implementation, and impact of the CDF principles.

Country Ownership

Conclusions: Governments and donors have expanded their consultation activities for the purpose of strategy formulation with key stakeholder groups in civil society and the private sector. This process has helped to strengthen ownership of reforms. But the ownership has been narrowly based when consultations have been confined to the executive branch of the government, supplemented by ad hoc consultations with organizations that donors or government choose. Selected interest groups have been given voice in these cases, while the wider public good—in the stewardship of elected representatives—has been overlooked. Parliaments and elements of civil society and the private sector have complained of being marginalized in the process (Burkina Faso, Uganda).

> Special efforts are needed to involve marginalized groups... and to take account of their views

An important lesson from the experience of CDF-style participatory consensus building is that in countries with credible representative institutions, it is desirable for the international development community to work through these institutions. But in order for parliaments and governments to exercise their stewardship and accountability functions, they need better information (such as PPAs) on the impacts of their decisions on different groups, particularly on the poorest, who normally have little or no voice.

Recommendation for recipient countries: *To enhance country ownership, government and parliament should consult among diverse interest groups.* This embraces the full range of civil society and the private sector, including those who lack an organized voice, such as the poorest and women. Several consultative approaches will be required.

Recommendation for all donors: *Work with the government in devising an approach for consultations with elected officials and nongovernment representatives.* The views of diverse interest groups, while valuable, do not sum to the public good. Donors should work with recipient authorities to establish the appropriate role for elected officials at the national and local levels and ensure they have access to meetings. In consultations with interest groups, special efforts are needed to involve marginalized groups, typically the poorest—particularly women—and private sector representatives, and to take account of their views. Materials and presentations should be easily understandable to all local audiences, particularly at the grassroots level. Donors should be prepared to provide assistance to strengthen the capacities of these groups to participate in strategy consultations.

Conclusion: Some elements of the PRSP process stand in the way of the principle of country ownership. For example, some country governments believe that the PRSP requires their development programs to focus too heavily on social expenditures. The fact that PRSPs must pass through the Boards of the Bank and the International Monetary Fundis also thought to limit countries' range of options. Evidence from some of the country case studies suggests that they resent what they see as Board "approval" of what is supposed to be a country-owned document, the PRSP.

Additional recommendations specifically for the World Bank:

1) *Clarify the Bank's openness to alternative PRSP-consistent development strategies.* Misperceptions of Bank policy could be mitigated by more openness by the Bank to

alternative and well-argued approaches to addressing poverty—for example, an approach that emphasizes strengthening basic infrastructure. The resulting strategy should be well buttressed by best practice retrospective and prospective participatory and analytical instruments.

2) *Differentiate more clearly the Board's roles in relation to the PRSP and the Country Assistance Strategy (CAS).* The Bank should seek to communicate more clearly and consistently the distinction between the Board's endorsement of the PRSP as a basis for concessional lending and its approval of strategies contained in the CAS. Careful wording in press releases following Board discussions can contribute to this, as well as clarifications of the issue in the context of in-country PRSP consultations.

Country-led Partnership

Conclusions: The "new paradigm" of country-led partnership is intended to give the recipient country a leading voice with respect to the quality of aid it is receiving. Progress has been highly uneven—across donors, across countries, across sectors within countries, and across the dimensions of the country-led partnership principle. Some donors in a number of countries have risen to the challenge—or used it to underpin ongoing efforts.[42] A few bilateral donors have done a better job than multilateral agencies; others have done worse.

Some recipient countries also are beginning to meet the challenge. Where this has happened, the quality of the aid program has improved. This is reflected in intermediate outcomes in some sectors in at least one country (primary school enrollment and access to safe water in Uganda).[43] Where SWAps have been under

way (for example, the Health SWAp in Ghana), sector strategies tend to be more coherent, and information flow, monitoring, and resource planning are better than in other sectors. But it is too soon to tell if there will be sustained improvement in higher-level development outcomes, such as educational attainment and health status.

Effective country leadership of aid partnerships has been difficult to achieve because of the asymmetries in the donor-recipient relationships. Some donors face domestic political resistance to reducing the use of international consultants and to harmonizing procedures. Reform will require both donors and recipient countries to make significant changes in their behaviors and processes, changes that may be in conflict with the political environments of donors. Although field initiatives, along with the quality of field staff and leadership, can influence donor headquarters, the basic parameters for donor behavior are set at the headquarters level. In-country initiatives have only rarely spearheaded changes in headquarters policies and practice. One of the means for donors to facilitate country leadership is to provide financial resources through mechanisms that apply common pool principles, such as budget support through Poverty Reduction Support Credits (PRSCs) and SWAps. At the same time, donors, because they are accountable for public funds, cannot accede to country leadership if recipient countries are perceived to be suffering from corruption, economic mismanagement, and weak public expenditure management and accountability. Causation can run in both directions: good country performance can encourage flexible financial support, i.e., budget support, and provision of flexible support facilitates country leadership. Both influences can be observed in Uganda's experience, but a modicum of country performance was required before significant flexible support was forthcoming.

Many countries will need capacity strengthening in order to fully assume leadership of aid management and coordination functions. But capacity development is a long process and cannot be effective as long as individual donors propose different and sometimes incompatible forms of support, each following different timetables and goals.

Recommendations for all donors: More impetus is needed to accelerate the alignment of assistance strategies with country strategies, information sharing between donors and partner countries, focused local capacity building with a long-term perspective, greater selectivity of donor-funded activities, and harmonization of donor procedures and practices. Donor-only coordination exercises, while they can constitute a first step toward harmonization, and may be the only option in immediate post-conflict and some low-income countries under stress (LICUS), do not by themselves foster recipient country ownership. A second step would be recipient country leadership in moving to greater strategic alignment, programmatic selectivity, and harmonization around country strategy, policies, standards, and procedures.

1) *Step back from micro-managing the aid process at the country level.* Country-led partnership implies that donors are prepared to step back from micro-managing the in-country aid process and aid relationships to give countries space to innovate and take risks, and to make mistakes and learn from them, and at the same time, provide the capacity building and resources countries need to fully take over aid management. This will require mutual trust and transparency on both sides.

2) *Give the recipient country voice and oversight over aid quality.* Changes in donor policies and practices require actions at the headquarters and international levels, as well as within recipient countries. The present unsatisfactory situation has continued for many years in spite of years of multidonor harmonization efforts (for example, to harmonize procurement). A challenge, therefore, for follow-up to the February 2003 Rome Conference and other harmonization initiatives will be to break from business as usual and introduce a new paradigm. This will involve giving the recipient country control it has not previously had. To strengthen the role of the country and to bolster accountability for achieving progress, one proposal is to establish a system of regular country-level review panels composed of independent reviewers representing the recipient country and donors. The panels would review donor as well as recipient country performance against a mutually agreed code of conduct and targets. Results would be accessible to the public and published regularly (e.g., for CG meetings).

3) *Decentralize staff and delegate more authority to the field.* Effective aid coordination at the country level requires that donor field offices have more flexibility and resources to foster recipient country leadership. To move in this direction, donors should provide their country field offices with enough delegated authority and resources to participate fully in pertinent country-led aid coordination activities. And they should select field staff who have proven partnership and relationship-building skills as well as the requisite subject area expertise. For smaller donors, greater selectivity may require them to specialize and upgrade their technical capacity.

4) *Plan for phase out of PIUs.* While a case can sometimes be made for temporary project implementation units (PIU) under conditions of weak government capacity, every PIU should be accompanied by a plan to phase out over the life of the project or program. Salary

incentives typically associated with PIUs are a thorny but critical issue for donor harmonization. Training and capacity building would normally accompany the phase out process, and, if needed, which is often the case, public service reform, including pay reform.

Additional recommendations specifically for the World Bank: The country case studies highlighted some aspects of these recommendations that apply in particular to the Bank.

1) *Continue decentralization and delegation of authority to field offices.* The Bank has made considerable progress in decentralization over the last five years. This has involved not only the placement of country directors in the field, but also the fielding of additional headquarters staff and decisionmaking authority.

2) *Select, train, and reward staff—in part—on the basis of their partnership performance.* This applies not only to field-based staff but also to headquarters staff who service country programs (e.g., sector specialists).

3) *Practice what the Bank preaches regarding harmonization and simplification, program or budget support, and selectivity and "stepping back."* Complexity of Bank procurement procedures was a common complaint heard by case study teams. Procedural simplification as well as harmonization are needed. Transparent and timely provision of documents should be the norm, given that difficulty in obtaining Bank strategy and procurement documents was cited in several case studies. The Bank often leads in providing flexible instruments, such as PRSCs and sector budget support, but the case studies show that this is not uniform practice. There is still a tendency for the Bank to involve itself in every sector. The CDF implies that it should cede donor leadership when others have comparative advantage.

Recommendations for recipient countries:

1) *Put responsibility for aid coordination at a high level of the government.* If countries are to grasp the leadership of development partnerships, they need to discourage fragmented, disparate relationships among individual donors and individual ministries and agencies within the recipient government. The aid management mechanism should be at the cabinet (or other high) level, to ensure cooperation across ministries—for example, at the level of the Minister of Finance and Planning. One indicator of strong leadership is when the government rejects any donor offers that do not fall within the national plan or MTEF.

2) *Implement and enforce procurement and other rules that will engender the confidence of donors.* Donors require confidence in the integrity and efficiency of the government's resource management systems, especially procurement and accounting and auditing. This is especially true if donors are to accelerate adoption of common pool funding mechanisms. One way to increase their confidence is to promulgate procurement and other rules that will meet donors' expectations, and to implement and enforce them consistently. Another way is to encourage civil society to help in reducing corruption by budget and implementation monitoring, promoting transparency, and educating the public.

The Road Ahead and an Opportunity

This evaluation concludes that progress in implementing the far-reaching changes posited by the CDF has been uneven, with the broadest progress occurring in countries that have been applying one or more of the CDF principles for a number of years. This finding is not surprising given that it is still early and the CDF principles are about changing norms, behaviors, and institutional practices—change that does not happen easily or overnight for either donors or recipient countries. Transparency and mutual trust are required of all parties. Therefore, continuous political leadership and sustained will by all major development actors are needed if today's dysfunctional aid practices are to be changed. If not, internal politics, incentives, and capacity constraints will continue to frustrate the emergence of the new behaviors that the CDF encourages.

Transparency and mutual trust are required of all parties

One area that needs more attention is the *relationship between the implementation of the CDF principles and certain sectors and segments of society.* The analysis summarized in Chapter 3 suggests that failure to involve adequately the private sector in CDF processes gives them little or no impact on the business environment in developing countries. Country case study evidence indicates that marginalized groups, such as the poorest and women, are not being adequately consulted in the formulation of development strategy.

The evaluation suggests several important areas that would benefit from expanded learning efforts, including research and exchange of experience:

■ How to establish country-owned monitoring and evaluation (M&E) systems that bring stakeholders together and build from innovations in government and civil society

■ How to start a debate in donor countries about agency incentives, public attitudes toward aid, pooling resources and results, and the role of Audit Offices and Treasuries in compounding the problem

■ How to expand learning *between* recipient countries—e.g., disseminating Uganda's experience with the MTEF to other countries.

Promising opportunities have recently emerged for donors and recipients to move ahead. For instance, on the harmonization of donor procedures and practices—a heretofore largely intractable component of the country-led partnership—a momentum for change is building. The consensus that emerged out of the Rome High-Level Forum on Harmonization (as contained in the Rome Declaration on Harmonization, February 2003) calls for donors and recipient countries to: (1) utilize and strengthen existing mechanisms to maintain peer pressure on implementing harmonization agreements; and (2) conduct stocktaking meetings in early 2005 in order to contribute to the review of Monterrey Consensus implementation. There are also a number of opportunities to bring the CDF principles into fuller implementation. These include following up with the New Partnership for African Development, the Monterrey and Rome consensuses, the ongoing work on harmonization of the SPA, and the World Bank's initiative on monitoring and measuring for results, including the increasing adoption of MDGs in PRSPs and other country development frameworks. A related ongoing effort is the development of a *Millennium Development Strategy.* The key elements of such a strategy are already to be found in the CDF and in the efforts of some countries to implement the CDF as a means to achieve the MDGs. The World Bank, in cooperation with other development partners, should play a lead role in integrating the CDF principles into these and other global initiatives.

The CDF Evaluation at a Glance

January 1999

World Bank President James D. Wolfensohn introduces the Comprehensive Development Framework (CDF).

Late 1999

The Operations Evaluation Department (OED) is asked by the Executive Board of the World Bank to conduct an evaluation of the implementation of the CDF. The Bank's Development Research Group (DECRG) also proposes conducting research on the CDF. The two units agree to participate in the CDF evaluation as a joint effort.

October 2000

The CDF evaluation is officially launched at a CDF Research Evaluation Workshop held on October 19 & 20, 2000, that brought together about 50 persons from CDF pilot countries, donors and other development agencies, NGOs, and academic institutions.

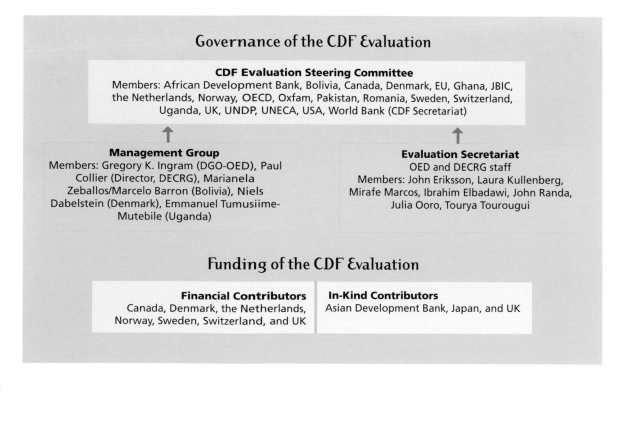

Governance of the CDF Evaluation

CDF Evaluation Steering Committee
Members: African Development Bank, Bolivia, Canada, Denmark, EU, Ghana, JBIC, the Netherlands, Norway, OECD, Oxfam, Pakistan, Romania, Sweden, Switzerland, Uganda, UK, UNDP, UNECA, USA, World Bank (CDF Secretariat)

Management Group
Members: Gregory K. Ingram (DGO-OED), Paul Collier (Director, DECRG), Marianela Zeballos/Marcelo Barron (Bolivia), Niels Dabelstein (Denmark), Emmanuel Tumusiime-Mutebile (Uganda)

Evaluation Secretariat
OED and DECRG staff
Members: John Eriksson, Laura Kullenberg, Mirafe Marcos, Ibrahim Elbadawi, John Randa, Julia Ooro, Tourya Tourougui

Funding of the CDF Evaluation

Financial Contributors
Canada, Denmark, the Netherlands, Norway, Sweden, Switzerland, and UK

In-Kind Contributors
Asian Development Bank, Japan, and UK

Products of the CDF Evaluation

Six Country Case Studies

Bolivia Country Case Study
Authors: N. Boesen,
L. Kullenberg,
J. A. Peres, J. C. Requena

Burkina Faso Country Case Study
Authors: D. Lallement,
D. McMillan, K. O'Sullivan,
P. Plane, K. Savadogo

Ghana Country Case Study
Authors: N. Boesen,
L. Kullenberg, T. Killick,
A. Oduro, M. Marcos

Romania Country Case Study
Authors: J. Eriksson,
L. Salinger, D. Sandu

Uganda Country Case Study
Authors: J. Eriksson,
R. Rwampororo, D. Pedley,
M. Marcos

Vietnam Country Case Study
Authors: A.J. Morten,
L. Kullenberg, R. Mallon,
K. Nishino, H.M. Tien

CDF Evaluation Synthesis Report

Authors:
J. Eriksson,
I. Elbadawi,
C. Lancaster,
A. Scott,
P. Collier,
L. Kullenberg,
C. Soludo,
M. Marcos

Advisors:
H. Kohama,
D. Pressley,
A. Scott,
S. Wangwe,
S. Maxwell

Cross-cutting Econometric Study
"Development Impact of CDF-like Strategies" by I. Elbadawi, G. Mavrotas, and J. Randa

Four Thematic Studies

Long-Term Holistic Framework
Authors: A. A. G. Ali,
A. Disch

Ownership and Participation
Authors: H. Handousa,
C. Lancaster

Country-led Partnership
Authors: T. Holmgren,
C. Soludo

Results Orientation
Authors: H. P. Hatry,
K. Yansane

Approach Paper for a Multi-Partner Evaluation of the Comprehensive Development Framework

Background

This paper describes the scope and basic components for a multi-partner, multi-country evaluation of the Comprehensive Development Framework (CDF). It is intended to serve as a basis for decisions by:

- CDF pilot and other countries to participate in the evaluation

- Development agencies to contribute financially and intellectually to the evaluation

- The Evaluation Steering Committee and the Board Committee on Development Effectiveness (CODE) of the World Bank to empower the Evaluation Management Group to prepare a detailed evaluation design.

The CDF comprises a set of principles that a number of developing countries and development assistance agencies have been seeking to put into practice over the last two years. Although the CDF, as such, was articulated by the World Bank President in January 1999, the principles on which it is based are distilled from development experience over the last five decades.[44]

In late 1999, CODE asked the Operations Evaluation Department (OED) to conduct an evaluation of the implementation of the CDF. At about the same time the Bank's Development Research Group (DECRG) proposed conducting research on the CDF. This led to an agreement by the two units to undertake the CDF evaluation as a joint effort. To launch and help guide the evaluation, about 50 persons from CDF pilot countries, donors and other development agencies, nongovernmental organizations, and academic institutions were invited to a workshop in Washington D.C. on October 19 and 20, 2000. A subsequent session on the CDF evaluation was held at the November 2000 meeting of the OECD/DAC Evaluation Working Party.

Based on the interest evinced at these meetings, 30 representatives of donors, developing countries, and other development organizations were invited to a meeting in Paris, January 16, 2001.[45] This group agreed to form a multi-partner CDF Evaluation Steering Committee. It confirmed that the design and governance of the evaluation should reflect the CDF principles of country ownership, country-led partnership, and participation, with full involvement of development agencies[46] and recipients, including civil society and the private sector. It also highlighted the need for a timely assessment of how CDF principles are being implemented within countries' development processes, taking full account of the Poverty Reduction Strategy Paper (PRSP) initiative.[47]

Objectives and Scope

The objectives of the evaluation are: (1) to assess how the CDF is being implemented on the ground; (2) to identify the factors that have facilitated implementation of CDF principles and those that have hindered it; and (3) to promote learning and capacity development in countries where CDF principles are being implemented. The evaluation will deal with the relevance, efficacy, and efficiency of the overall development assistance system in selected countries, both on the ground and at the policy level, including linkages to the international development assistance architecture and the *International Development Goals* (IDGs).

A characterization of the four CDF principles and some of their properties is given in box A2-1. The elaboration of these principles continues to evolve. There is no authoritative set of definitions. This evaluation itself should help to refine their meaning.

The evaluation will consist of the following main components:

- Case studies of five CDF pilot countries and one non-CDF pilot country

- Five thematic studies and a cross-cutting econometric study

- An overall synthesis study.

The primary target audiences for the evaluation are the key government, donor, civil society, and private sector stakeholders in the case study countries, and senior managements and governing authorities of development agencies. Secondary target audiences are stakeholders in other developing countries, and tertiary audiences are the taxpaying citizens of all countries.

The primary orientation of the evaluation is on *self-evaluation and learning*. All main actors and their behavior, processes, and practices with respect to CDF implementation will be subject to evaluative review, whether donors, governments, civil society, or private sector. The evaluation will seek to model sustainable ways of implementing the CDF principles.[48]

The Functionality of CDF Implementation: A "Balance Sheet" Approach

The CDF principles as outlined in box A2-1 have achieved broad acceptance. The evaluation will ascertain whether they have been practiced and, if so, whether the ways in which they have been implemented have been functional for pursuing overarching development objectives, such as the IDGs.[49] This requires an identification of the possible benefits and costs of CDF implementation. Twelve potential benefits and ten potential costs are suggested in box A2-2. This list is not exhaustive; it will be expanded and refined for the evaluation design. The benefits and costs will be framed as hypotheses with associated "tests," or evaluation questions.

A Logical Framework for the CDF Principles

The employment of a "log frame" helps to clarify how the CDF principles contribute to higher-order development objectives. *Inputs* are the actions taken and costs incurred by partners to create a holistic, long-term development framework, and to improve the country ownership, country-led partnership, and results orientation of poverty reduction

Box. A2-1. The Principles of the Comprehensive Development Framework

I. Long-term, Holistic Development Framework
Addressing a country's development priorities requires a strong anchor in an appropriate, consistent, long-term vision of its needs and ways to address them. The vision also needs to be holistic; that is, it needs to:

- Be all-encompassing, taking into account simultaneously the key economic and financial issues, the requirements of structural change, the social issues, and other factors impinging on the country's social and economic development

- Cover the inter-linkages between sectors, since success in one sector is often linked integrally to progress in others.

Development interventions funded by the government and donors need to be carefully reviewed and appropriately sequenced in order to obtain the optimal mix of policies, programs, and instruments within an overall hard budget constraint.

II. Country Ownership
The country needs to be in the driver's seat, owning and directing the development agenda with the support of all other actors. The executive branch of government, therefore, needs to build consensus internally within the government, including the legislative structures and all other levels of government, and to consult with all stakeholders outside government, including the private sector and other elements of civil society, as well as with the country's external partners. The purpose of such consultation is to draw out ideas, knowledge, and opinions and to promote the broadening of consensus on the strategy expressed in the long-term, holistic vision. Enabling such ownership will often require strengthening of capacity in government and elsewhere in society.

III. Country-led Partnership
Enabling the country to be in the driver's seat requires strong partnership among the executive branch of government, other levels of government, the legislature, local authorities, civil society, the private sector, donors, international agencies, and other development actors. Such partnership should:

- Bring together, within a single framework, under government leadership, analytical and diagnostic work.

- Align donor actions to the national strategy and promote selectivity to avoid duplication.

- Reduce wasteful competition.

- Encourage common procedures among all development partners.

- Support the government's lead in managing aid coordination.

IV. Results Orientation
A country's national vision needs to link its overall aim to concrete development results, in a way in which progress toward the aims of that vision can be assessed. These development results are those sought through a broad-based national dialogue process. Since a key aim of the CDF is more effective and sustainable poverty reduction, the specific development results sought should be guided and informed by the *Millennium Development Goals* (MDGs), which have largely emerged from agreements in U.N. conferences during the 1990s.

Source: Drawn in part from World Bank 2000a, pp. 80-81.

Box A2-2. A Balance Sheet Approach to Evaluating the CDF: An Illustration

Potential Benefits of CDF Implementation

Long-term, Holistic Development Framework

- The CDF focus on results, the long term, and a holistic vision promotes the quality of development policy and strategic planning and the link between planning and budgeting.
- This focus also improves the quality of public expenditures, and the capacity for public expenditure management and sustainable resource management in countries.

Country Ownership

- The CDF fosters country ownership, based on "rules of the game" that are mutually agreed by development partners and are facilitated by changed behavior on the part of IFIs, bilateral donors, and other development agencies to create space for ownership.
- Such ownership, in turn, leads to better policies and processes than old-style conditionality (e.g., geared to greater equity and faster poverty reduction because of more inclusive decisionmaking).
- Holistic approaches have led to a better combination of quantitative and qualitative assessments of poverty in decisionmaking and policymaking.
- The CDF leads to broad-based ownership, anchored around the legislature in a democratic system, that recognizes other stakeholders (such as the civil service, NGOs, business and professional groups), as well as the need for greater political independence of some institutions (e.g., the central bank).
- Broad-based ownership leads to less policy reversal, better implementation, and better policy design.
- Vulnerable and marginalized groups, women in particular, have been better represented and more involved as a result of implementation of CDF principles.

Country-led Partnership

- The CDF matrix—the categories in the rows (sectors) and columns (development actors and part-ners) and their degree of aggregation—can influence the incentives for development agencies in a way that fosters collective actions among them in a context of partnership.
- Implementation of the country-led partnership principle will result in greater coherence and efficiency (lower transaction costs) of aid programs.

Results Orientation

- In turn, the ensuing new aid regime will enhance accountability and good governance.
- A results focus leads to a more flexible and immediate means for citizens to be involved in providing direct feedback on the quality of government-provided services.

Potential Costs of CDF Implementation

Country Ownership

- Enhanced ownership may lead to programs that sharply violate some broadly accepted develop-ment policies, and "old-style" conditionality may be the only alternative acceptable to donors.
- To the extent that there are only a few governments involved in the CDF, yardstick convergence generated by peer pressure may not be possible to realize under broadly based ownership.

Box A2-2, continued...

- Similarly, country capacity may be so weak under some conditions (for example, conflict and post-conflict countries) that reliance on country ownership will need to be circumscribed.

- The implementation of CDF principles may be perceived by civil society organizations as being imposed by donors.

- Broader participation could result in loss of prioritization; diluted role of professional expertise; and/or undue influence of narrow but well-organized lobbies.

- The CDF may tend to undermine sustainability of growth, because more inclusive decisionmaking might make it harder to sustain growth-enhancing policies.

- Broad-based participation could be very time- and transactions-intensive.

Country-led Partnership

- Greater emphasis on partnership could result in higher transaction costs of aid delivery if development agency partners do not agree to harmonize procedures and conditionality.

- Closer alignment of donor and governmental priorities could come at the expense of civil society–government relations.

- With intensified coordination, major donors may still not adequately consult relevant stakeholders.

Results Orientation

- Could lead to excessive focus on indicators and bureaucratic proliferation of "score cards."

programs. *Outputs* are the changed behaviors of partners, reflecting the CDF principles. The *purposes* are the country-enabling conditions, as reflected in country-level policy, institutional, and aid quality *outcome indicators*. Goals are measured by *impact indicators* defined case by case in light of the International Development Goals (IDGs). The assumptions on the basis of which the results chain is constructed will be specified in each case. The log frames will help to connect the balance sheet approach with the aid quality considerations, e.g., the role of country ownership in improving development results (a balance sheet type of analysis) will depend in part on whether aid flows are influenced by the policy environment (an aid quality consideration). Costs and benefits and core evaluation questions will emerge from the log frames. The Design Paper will fully articulate four log frames, one for each of the CDF principles, and show how they feed into higher-level purposes and goals, thus comprising a composite log frame.

Other Methodological Considerations

Country-specific and thematic studies will be guided by the same conceptual model. This will enhance cross-fertilization and comparability, though there will be room for useful differentiation in terms of methodology of analysis, and tailor-made features will be introduced to respond to individual country needs. Initial results of the thematic studies, which will be desk studies, will be shared with the country case study teams for potential in-depth exploration.

Additional features of the design and methodology for the evaluation will be covered in the detailed Design Paper to be developed as a next step in the process, taking full account of comments made by Steering Committee members. For example, an aspect that will be addressed in the Design Paper is the potential *interrelationships* among CDF principles and the possibility that certain sequences may be associated with more lasting impact than others (e.g., country ownership before other principles). The evaluation itself is expected to illuminate such relationships. The methodology will be subject to further refinement during the early stages of implementation of the country and thematic studies, as indicated below.

Country Case Studies

Country studies will review the experience of five CDF pilot countries and one non-CDF pilot country where one or more CDF principles have been applied.[50] Given the short period of time since the CDF has been consciously implemented, it will not be possible for the country studies to assess the *impacts* of CDF implementation on the overarching development goals represented by the IDGs. However, the country reviews will throw light on the evaluability of individual CDF programs in terms of the linkages intended by stakeholders between CDF processes and priority development goals. A main focus of the country studies will, as explained above, be on changes observed in *outcomes, outputs,* and *inputs* in connection with the extent and quality of implementation of the CDF principles. Some of these changes should favor positive development impacts, while others could be inimical to development given the tensions (along with the synergies) that have been shown to exist among the CDF principles.

The country studies will not constitute "country evaluations" as normally undertaken by the World Bank and other development agencies, although they will draw on relevant methodologies to assess the performance of development actors. They will be planned and designed in full consultation with country authorities in order to reflect their special interests and their individual circumstances. To the full extent feasible, they will be implemented with participation from the various partners active in the country—government, civil society, the private sector, donors, and other development agencies. These stakeholders will constitute a country steering committee for each case study. The aim will be to initiate a process that informs decisionmakers and leads to institutional change in support of poverty reduction.

The selection of case study countries will be mainly determined by the interest of the country concerned and its development partners to participate actively in the evaluation. Other selection criteria will include maintaining balance in terms of Regional coverage and avoiding overlap with other related evaluative efforts, such as the ongoing SPA-sponsored country case studies of PRSP implementation in eight African countries and the UNECA "PRSP Learning Group" initiative. At least one non-PRSP CDF pilot country will be included.

The first field visit to a country will consist of a scoping mission of one or two persons, including at least one member of the evaluation secretariat team. They will work with the country steering committee and a local institution to:[51]

■ Agree on the detailed terms-of-reference and implementation modalities for the country study.

■ Assemble and analyze pertinent literature, documents, and data sources.

- Design questionnaire surveys of key stake-holders to be subsequently administered by the local institution.

- Design key informant and focus group interview protocols for the second visit.[52]

- Plan and make arrangements for a more extensive second visit, to take place four to six weeks after the first visit (after the results of the questionnaire surveys are available).

The second field visit will be composed of two-to-three highly qualified professionals, drawn from, or representing, the key development agencies active in the country. They will join with a local team composed of a like number of individuals drawn from the local steering committee and/or local partner institution. The combined team should be skilled at facilitating interviews and workshops, as well as having good analytical skills. They will conduct key informant and focus group interviews and analyze the results of the various data sources, including surveys. Meetings or workshops will be held with key stakeholders, including decisionmakers, to discuss and validate the findings of the analyses of surveys, interviews, and other data sources, drawing out their policy and programmatic implications. The roles of *all* partners in the development of the country, including donors and other development agencies, will be assessed through these data-gathering and workshop activities. Senior officials of the main donors and development agencies will be invited to join decisionmaker-level workshops during the last day or two of this second mission—or perhaps slightly after the mission, when a draft report is ready.

An important value expected to be achieved is the learning that will take place through the process, including the nurturing of domestic monitoring and evaluation capacity development. Another objective will be to encourage

the creation of an ongoing mechanism for periodic assessment of CDF processes and feedback to decisionmakers.

In those countries where PRSPs have been or are being prepared, the relationships between the CDF and the PRSP will be explored, taking into account the early stage of PRSPs. A thorough review will be made of ongoing PRSP monitoring efforts, such as those conducted under the auspices of the Strategic Partnership with Africa (SPA) and the U.N. Economic Commission for Africa (UNECA). The objective will be to avoid duplication and to explore possibilities for complementarity and cooperation.[53] The CDF evaluation should help define the methods and processes for an in-depth PRSP evaluation at a later stage of PRSP implementation.

Thematic Studies

Six thematic studies are proposed: one on each of the four CDF principles; one on CDF-PRSP linkages; and a paper that will attempt a cross-country econometric analysis. These studies will give particular attention to the impact on aid effectiveness of donor and development agency behavior as reflected in their policies, procedures, and practices.[54]

Although the CDF as such was introduced only recently, its principles were previously practiced at various times in different countries. Therefore, the cross-country analysis will measure whether countries and development agencies that practiced something close to the CDF principles performed better (in terms of processes and outcomes) than countries and agencies that did not. The method for testing this hypothesis will utilize a modified-control-group model. The analysis will require indicators of "closeness" to CDF principles, processes, intermediate outcomes, and development impacts. The log frames, to be developed more fully in the Design Paper, will help to guide these analyses. Examples of types of indicators to be used and/or developed for each of the four principles follow.

■ *Long-term, holistic development framework.* Indicators of country priorities, as well as sector balance, will be derived from various sources, including the Bank's Social and Structural Reviews (SSRs). This will permit testing whether countries where these priorities were part of a long-term, holistic vision performed better.

■ *Country ownership.* Indicators of country ownership have been developed by OED. These will be adapted to assess the conditions under which greater ownership leads to better results. Equally, the extent of participation can be approximated by governance indicators being developed.

■ *Country-led partnership.* Various proxies have been proposed for the quality of partnership and of aid coordination. For example, indicators of extent of tied aid, project vs. program aid, and harmonization of development agency processes will be used to examine the linkage of these factors to outcomes.

■ *Results orientation.* Indicators of focus on poverty reduction and other related dimensions of development outcomes and impacts, availability of long-term development frameworks, and learning from results will be developed and tested for both countries and agencies.

The first four papers will focus on developing detailed indicators of "functionality" for these principles; while the fifth paper will address linkages to the PRSPs. The overarching development objective of achieving a meaningful and lasting impact on poverty would be a cross-cutting issue in all four of the CDF principles

papers. At the same time, a dedicated thematic paper on CDF-PRSP linkages would make a distinctive contribution. While it will be important to analyze the linkages between the CDF and PRSPs in each of the four papers, these by themselves would be rather limited and partial analyses because they would be focusing on the marginal effects of individual CDF principles. A thematic paper focusing on CDF-PRSP linkages could provide a valuable input to the World Bank and other multilateral and bilateral development institutions as they strive to ensure that the PRSP initiative is appropriately situated in a context of a holistic development vision.

The sixth paper will attempt to link the range of intermediate outcomes and processes identified in the first five papers to key development impacts. Several indicators of development impacts will be used, including aggregate measures, such as GDP per capita; distributional indicators, such as the income of the bottom quintile; and, where available, other indicators of well being, such as infant mortality, life expectancy, and educational attainment. To facilitate comparison, among the indicators to be employed will be those also used to measure progress toward the International Development Goals. The focus of this paper will therefore be to assess the functionality of the four CDF principles as a means for testing their potential influence on development impacts. The main elements of the methodology are:

i. Analysis of association/correlation among functional indicators of CDF and development outcomes and impacts:

■ Hypothesis on possible association/correlation (though not necessarily causation)

■ Corresponding preliminary methods of analysis

■ The potential value of the exercise for the country-specific case studies.

ii. Estimating the marginal contribution of the CDF:

▪ Framework for analyzing the marginal contribution of a CDF-like environment to development, controlling for the counterfactual of "what would the treatment country have done without the CDF-like experience"

▪ Potential implications of the results for the country-specific case studies.

The Design Paper will elucidate additional technical details of the methodology to be employed in the analysis.

The foregoing suggests the following implications for analyzing the impact of CDF implementation on development outcomes:

▪ Processes and intermediate outcomes of CDF implementation are inseparable from the task of evaluating its effect on development impacts.[55]

▪ Development partners are often faced with real tradeoffs when, for example, country ownership produces programs that donors and development agencies find difficulty agreeing with.[56]

▪ Adoption/implementation of CDF principles is also influenced by the initial conditions relating to development performance, intermediate outcomes, and processes, among others.

▪ The analysis should be placed in a broader and more dynamic context that accounts for the process of learning and capacity building as the CDF proceeds.

Assessing the Quality of Aid

Recent research and policy work on development aid has focused on the importance of a good policy environment for aid effectiveness. However, effectiveness is also constrained by the quality of aid, including its instruments, delivery mechanisms for knowledge and resources, and donor coordination. Recipients and development agencies have a mutual responsibility for development outcomes and the distinctive accountabilities and reciprocal obligations of all parties. This is all the more important given that the developing countries and regions where poverty is the highest and institutions are the weakest, are also the ones that are likely to be the most aid-dependent. Although it is clearly not the only consideration, improvements in the quality of aid in these countries can make a critical contribution to achieving the levels of growth required for poverty reduction on a sustained basis. Unfortunately, these countries commonly experience what might be characterized as an "aid-bombardment" syndrome.[57] This syndrome (an unintended consequence of poor aid coordination) is apparent in countries in which the sheer volume of resources and numbers of development agencies, activities, and complex and inconsistent procedural requirements overwhelm the government's capacity to plan, budget, manage, monitor, and evaluate.

Meaningful improvement in aid quality will require greater coherence, selectivity, and efficiency in development agency support of country development strategies. It will also require more effective support for capacity strengthening so that recipient countries with a sound policy framework can assume greater leadership and responsibility for the management and coordination of aid resources. Success in tackling these issues cannot be achieved solely at the country level; actions are also required at the headquarters levels of development agencies. Therefore, both the country and thematic studies of the CDF evaluation will examine the quality of country-led partnerships and their relationship to mandated aid procedures and to development

Box A2-3. Global and Country-Level Partnership Issues

Expanding country-led partnerships and participation. Partnerships, coordination, and dialogue are needed to build consensus on coherent programs. How do donors translate the concepts of partnership and participation into decisions on aid allocations—including to countries with views on development that differ from theirs? How do donors interact with civil society and with representative institutions—particularly parliaments—in ways that ensure they are well informed and properly involved in aid programs and processes and yet respect local institutions, policies, and processes? How might a "code of conduct" help?

Reducing aid delivery transactions costs. Harmonizing aid delivery policies and procedures, so as to reduce the heavy burden they often impose on poor countries, may well require development agencies to seek changes from their authorizing environments. To what extent are they prepared to do this?

Strengthening capacity and fostering country ownership. Are development agencies prepared to support programs for skills retention rather than for expatriate technical assistance? Are they willing to support comprehensive multi-donor programs and not fragmented programs that tend to undermine capacity (e.g., with their own administrative procedures and implementation units, ad hoc budgets, etc.)?

Decentralizing development. Many countries are devolving greater responsibilities and authority to local governments and communities so as to be more responsive to the needs of the poor. How can aid agencies support this process and at the same time strengthen the capacity of local entities to manage development programs?

Moving beyond boundaries. Aid mechanisms mostly focus on countries, but the twenty-first century will see a growing need for a range of international and regional public goods (e.g., in the areas of agricultural research, vaccine development, knowledge creation and acquisition, and conflict management). How should mechanisms for regional aid delivery be enhanced to support such efforts?

Enhancing debt relief. It is well established that high indebtedness reduces the quality of aid and perpetuates aid dependency. Excessive debt creates expectations of future taxes and policy reversals, which reduce the incentives for current investment. High fixed debt service obligations increase countries' leverage and raise uncertainty, especially if donor funding is decided on a short-term basis. Has incremental debt relief through the "HIPC" initiative proceeded at a sufficient pace to make a meaningful impact?

What basis for selectivity? Reallocating aid toward countries that are poor but maintain good policies would increase the development effectiveness of aid. In the past donors have undermined incentives by providing aid even when conditions are unfavorable. Is assistance being allocated on a more selective basis?

Moving away from aid dependence. Though aid cannot be phased out rapidly, plans should be made to free countries from aid dependence. Such plans need to be endorsed by recipients and their development partners and anchored in mutually agreed strategies of making recipient countries economically competitive and reducing poverty. What role can donors and development agencies, including the World Bank, play in supporting the agenda of poor countries in the WTO to ensure that WTO rule making mechanisms are made compatible with the development requirements of poor countries?

Source: Adapted from OED 1999; World Bank 2000d.

effectiveness on the ground. In this connection, ongoing work of the OECD Development Assistance Committee (DAC), such as its Peer Reviews and the new Bilateral Task Force on Donor Practices, is particularly relevant.

A range of partnership and aid quality issues at the country and global levels are presented in box A2-3. While such issues as those dealing with international public goods, debt relief, and trade cannot be covered in depth in this evaluation, they do relate to aid effectiveness. These linkages will be examined in the country and thematic studies where relevant.

Synthesis Report

Cross-cutting conclusions and lessons will be drawn from the country studies and thematic studies and presented in an overall synthesis report. Based on these conclusions, the report will frame recommendations for consideration by members of the Steering Committee and the entities they represent.

Dissemination Strategy

The workshops will be a major dissemination vehicle for the country studies. A dissemination strategy for the final products, such as the overall Synthesis Report and selected thematic and country studies, is an important issue that will be addressed in the Design Paper. The proposed budget provides for a workshop in late calendar 2002 to discuss the main findings and conclusions of the Synthesis Report.

CDF Principles: Working Definitions

The following "working definitions" are drawn from President Wolfensohn's January 19, 1999, speech launching the CDF, and documents subsequently issued by the CDF Secretariat (see World Bank 2001c).

Long-term, Holistic Development Framework

1) Design of 15-to-20 year vision statement containing monitorable development goals that:

   a. Take account of broad aspirations of the population

   b. Include sustainable poverty reduction as the overarching goal and related subgoals aligned with the Millennium Development Goals.

2) Formulation of a coherent medium-term (3-to-5 year) strategy for making progress toward vision goals, specifically addressing need for:

   a. Balance among macroeconomic and financial issues and structural and social concerns

   b. Priorities in the face of capacity and hard budget constraints; and time-bound, concrete actions, with attention to phasing and sequencing.

Country Ownership

1) Identification of development goals and formulation of strategy by the country, not by the donors.

2) Regular, broad-based stakeholder participation, under government leadership, including civil society, the private sector, local governments, and parliaments, with sustained public support from top political leadership and intellectual conviction by key policymakers, and strong links to institutions.

Country-led Partnership

1) Government leadership in management and coordination of development partners and aid resources, including:

   a. Consultative groups, donor roundtables, and other coordination mechanisms

   b. Analytical and diagnostic work

   c. Alignment of external support—including lending, grants, analytical and diagnostic work, and capacity building—with country's development strategy and donor comparative advantage

   d. Harmonization of development agency procedures and practices

   e. Alignment of internal partners' (civil society, the private sector, local governments) activities with the country's development strategy.

2) Relations among government, development agencies, other stakeholders, marked by:

   a. Mutual trust, consultation, and transparency

b. Assumption of mutual accountabilities and review of partners' performance

c. Demand-led support for strengthening government management and coordination capacity.

Results Orientation

1) Designing programs with evaluable objectives that contribute to development framework goals, and developing intermediate indicators toward these goals.

2) Monitoring and regularly sharing progress, with accountability for outcomes and goals, not just inputs.

3) Creating and enabling capacities to generate, monitor, and use results information to improve performance in achieving goals and accountability.

The CDF and the PRSP: Key Facts

Chronology of Events Leading to the CDF and PRSP

1980s

Era of structural adjustment. Aid conditioned on recipient government agreeing to change policies and/or institutions.

1990s

Widespread concerns about effectiveness and outcomes of aid. Mounting criticism of structural adjustment and lack of development progress in Sub-Saharan Africa.

Mid-1990s

Donors launch programs to increase aid effectiveness, including:

- First HIPC initiative (1996), IDGs (precursor to MDGs), OECD-DAC Partnership Forums, U.N. Development Assistance Framework.

- "Results Management" spreads from corporate world to development community (IDGs contribute to prominence of results focus in the CDF).

1994-95

U.N. sponsors series of international conferences that produced targets for socioeconomic change. Includes Population Conference in Cairo (1994); Social Development, Copenhagen (1995); Women, Beijing (1995).

1996

DAC members accept U.N. targets for socioeconomic change as IDGs (see *Shaping the 21st Century*, OECD/DAC 1996).

1998

New paradigm for development processes emerging at World Bank. Board agrees to ideas and approaches proposed in Partnerships Paper produced by newly formed Partnerships Group.

1998 Annual Meetings

World Bank President invites recipient countries to pilot "new development framework" (subsequently changed to Comprehensive Development Framework, as below).

January 1999

World Bank President proposes Comprehensive Development Framework (CDF) to address shortcomings in aid management to meet the challenge of equitable, sustainable development and poverty alleviation. CDF stresses process as well as content, including the idea that the *way aid is delivered* as well as the *content of aid funded activities* determines its effectiveness.

March 1999

Thirteen countries agree to become CDF pilot countries, with progress to be monitored and reviewed in September 2000. World Bank forms CDF Secretariat to track progress and disseminate good practice experience. In April 1999, the Development Committee supports the CDF approach.[58]

Sept. 1999
IMF/Bank launch Enhanced HIPC and PRSP. PRSP introduced as a medium-term strategy and expenditure program to be developed as a requirement for HIPC funds and to be prepared eventually by all IDA countries. The Development Committee decides that PRSPs should be based on CDF principles.

2000
U.N. accepts IDGs, with additions, as Millennium Development Goals (MDGs).

MDGs subsequently endorsed by most donors, including World Bank.

April 2000
IMF Managing Director and World Bank President issue joint statement signaling that PRSPs reflect CDF principles and provide the framework for IMF/Bank collaboration.

2001/2002
Recipient countries develop home-grown visions for improving aid effectiveness.

Newly created New Partnership for African Development (NEPAD) calls for joint responsibility, collective action, and peer pressure among African countries to enhance development effectiveness. By October 2002, 20 countries have produced full PRSPs and a further 29 have produced interim PRSPs (I-PRSPs).

Several bilateral donor policies reflect CDF principles (DFID, CIDA, and the like) and pres-

idents of multilateral development banks issue joint statement endorsing CDF.

PRSP: Principles, Elements, and Documentation

Definition
Country-produced paper outlining the government's strategy for reducing poverty. Updated every 2-5 years. The basis for HIPC initiative assistance and other concessional assistance from the World Bank, the IMF, and other donors.

Basic principles
Country-owned process, with broad-based participation, comprehensive focus, long-term perspective, and results oriented. Partnerships among government, domestic stakeholders, and donors.

Key elements
Country ownership built through a national participatory process; comprehensive poverty diagnosis; priority public actions; targets, indicators, and monitoring.

PRSP documentation

(a) Interim-PRSP
Document that presents a road map of progress toward PRSP preparation. Includes a statement of government commitment to poverty reduction; the main elements of the planned PRS and participatory process; a 3-year macroeconomic framework and policy matrix. If eligible, endorsement of the I-PRSP triggers HIPC decision point and interim HIPC debt relief.

(b) PRSP preparation status report
Expected one year after endorsement of the I-PRSP, to explain why more than one year is required to complete the PRSP and to identify any necessary technical assistance.

(c) PRSP

The full country-produced PRSP covering the four key elements outlined above. Required for HIPC debt relief, the PRGF, CAS, and PRSC.

(d) Annual PRSP Progress Report

Short document outlining progress in implementing the PRSP, including any achievements, shortfalls, or revisions to the strategy.

In HIPC-eligible cases, the first report triggers HIPC completion point.

(e) Joint Staff Assessments

Assessments by Fund and Bank staff as to whether the PRSP documentation presented to their Executive Boards constitutes (or promises to be, or continues to be) a sound basis for concessional assistance. Varies slightly according to what type of documentation is presented, i.e., (a)–(d) above.

(f) JSA Guidelines

Guidance to Bank and Fund staffs on the kinds of criteria to be used in assessing PRSP documents. No requirements as to content.

CDF-PRSP-CAS Link

Comprehensive Development Framework (CDF)

Long-term, Holistic Vision ⟷ Country Ownership ⟷ Partnership ⟷ Development Outcomes

Local Knowledge and Analyses
U.N. Common Country Assessment
World Bank Group Advice and Analysis
Other Partners' Advice and Analysis

Millennium Development Goals

Country Strategy Paper/Poverty Reduction Strategy Paper (PRSP)

Business Plan

ACTIVITY MATRIX	Structural/ Institutional	Social/ Human	Physical/ Rural/Urban	Macroeconomic/ Financial	Business Plan
Government					→ Expenditure Framework
World Bank Group					→ CAS
Private Sector					→ Investments
NGOs					→ Plans
Regional Development Banks					→ Business Plan
United Nations					→ UNDAF
IMF					→ PRGF
Bilaterals					→ Business Plan
EU					→ Country Strategy

Mid-term Strategy Implementation/Evaluation/Learning

PRSP: Poverty Reduction Strategy Paper CAS: Country Assistance Strategy UNDAF: UN Development Assistance Framework PRGF: Poverty Reduction and Growth Facility

Source: CDF Secretariat, World Bank.

Evaluation Methodology

The *Synthesis Report* draws from evaluative work and analysis of CDF implementation undertaken in the context of three main tasks:

I.   Case studies of five CDF pilot countries (Bolivia, Ghana, Romania, Uganda, Vietnam) and one non-CDF pilot country (Burkina Faso)

II. Four thematic studies

III. A cross-country econometric study.

Selection of Countries for Case Studies

The following six countries were selected for in-depth case studies: Bolivia, Ghana, Romania, Uganda, Vietnam (all CDF pilot countries) and Burkina Faso (non-CDF pilot). Selection was determined in the first instance by a country's desire to participate in the evaluation and by the willingness of the World Bank Resident Mission to facilitate. Priority was given to former CDF pilots with the most implementation experience and highest performance rankings (according to the CDF Secretariat) on grounds that these cases would offer the greatest potential for learning. One non-CDF pilot country was chosen as a control.

Because the PRSP is defined as an instrument for implementing the CDF principles, all countries selected (except Romania) were also PRSP countries. Consideration was also given to Regional balance and avoiding overlap with similar evaluative efforts (such as the SPA study of PRSP implementation in eight African countries).

The budget for the case studies was predetermined, so the inclusion of more than six cases, while desirable, would have been at the expense of depth. Other configurations were considered; for example, three CDF pilot and three non-CDF pilot, or three PRSP and three non-PRSP countries. However, the first alternative would have reduced the weight given to learning from the CDF pilot experiences, and the second would have shifted the balance toward countries where aid plays a smaller role relative to other sources of development finance. In the end, given that the primary purpose of the evaluation was to look at implementation issues, the Management Group and Steering Committee decided that selecting the longest running and best performing CDF pilots, together with one non-CDF pilot, was the optimal approach for generating the type and quantity of data required. (A discussion of sampling strategy choices is found in the GAO guidelines for Case Study Evaluations (GAO 1990). The basic argument is that cases should correspond closely to the focus of the evaluation and the evaluative question being asked. In other words, if you are interested in learning from implementation experience, you need to go countries with the longest track record of implementation.

How Country Studies Were Conducted

Country studies were carried out in two phases, a preparatory mission followed by intensive fieldwork. During the preparatory mission the evaluation was planned and designed in consultation with country authorities and donor representatives in order to reflect individual country interests and circumstances. Small focus group meetings were convened to propose and test key evaluation questions, taking as a point of departure the questions in the Design Paper (see World Bank 2001c). In each country, priority themes as well as sectors were identified (e.g., public sector reform, health, decentralization). Interviews were conducted in country capitals and selected districts, municipalities, and project sites. The evaluation teams typically included a representative from OED, and a combination of national and international consultants. In some cases, such as Vietnam, additional consultants and agency staff were provided by interested donors (for example, Japan MOFA/JBIC, ADB). DFID provided an agency staff member for the Uganda team.

In sum, the evaluation was carried out in a "CDF fashion" and involved a wide a range of stakeholders engaged in development work (from the policy level down to implementation of projects). These included representatives from national and local governments, donor agencies, mass organizations, the private sector, national NGOs, legislatures, academia, civil society organizations, and international NGOs. In each case study, a small group of advisors was selected from the various stakeholder groups and asked to serve as a *country reference group*, whose job was to guide the evaluation process and provide feedback on design choices and early findings. The evaluation teams were to have met periodically with the country reference groups to share preliminary observations with donors and national stakeholders in a closing workshop.

Types of Activities

A variety of activities and evaluation tools were employed during the course of the evaluation. These were:

- **Literature reviews.** Teams assembled and analyzed pertinent literature, documents, and data sources, and key country reports were posted on the CDF Evaluation Web site.

- **Questionnaire surveys** of key stakeholders. When possible these were designed in-country and administered by local institutions. In Vietnam, a local consulting firm distributed surveys to 290 Vietnamese and expatriate development practitioners about how they perceived changes in ODA management with reference to the CDF principles. One-hundred and seven people responded, of whom about 75 percent were Vietnamese from government and non-state agencies, and 25 percent were expatriates from donor agencies and international NGOs. In Burkina Faso, a survey was administered to a sample of local government officials, civil society representatives, and the private sector in four districts of varying socioeconomic levels, and got a good response rate of roughly 75 percent. In Romania the response rate relative to the sample design exceeded 100 percent for a survey administered to 722 experts and decisionmakers throughout the country who deal with development issues. In Bolivia detailed questions were sent to international agencies before the start of the evaluation. In Uganda, a survey was administered in a group meeting of stakeholders from government, civil society, and the private sector. An analysis of the 33 completed questionnaires formed the basis for subsequent workshops with parliamentarians and questionnaire respondents.

- **Structured interviews** were conducted with representatives from national and local governments, donor agencies, mass organizations, private sector leaders, national NGOs, legislatures, academia, civil society organizations, and international NGOs. Between 70 and 84 interviews (group and individual) were conducted per country, resulting in an average of roughly 145 people interviewed in each country.

■ Focus groups were organized based on sectors, themes (e.g., health, institutional reform), and professional affiliation (e.g., ministry staff, private sector, church).

■ Field trips to selected districts, municipalities, and project sites were made in all countries and included interviews with local government officials and politicians, project managers, operational NGOs, donor agencies, and municipal or district council members.

■ Closing workshops were held with key stakeholders and decisionmakers to discuss the team's preliminary findings. These workshops also served to draw out the policy and programmatic implications of the findings.

A survey on changes and trends in government-donor relations was carried out in Bolivia, Ghana, Romania, Uganda, and Vietnam as a specific parallel exercise to track progress in aid delivery and management practices. The survey results identify, and to the extent possible quantify, the impact on governments of donor procedural requirements, and the "transaction costs" they imply. A total of 17 bilateral and 9 multilateral donors across 5 CDF case study countries responded to the survey that was administered between May and September 2002. Local consultants administered the surveys in Bolivia, Romania, Uganda, and Vietnam. In Ghana and Romania, the surveys were followed up by interviews with donors and key government representatives. Table A5-1 lists the bilateral and multilateral donors that participated in the survey.

Thematic and Cross-Country Studies

There are four thematic studies, one on each of the four CDF principles. The fifth study undertakes a cross-country econometric analysis on CDF implementation and potential development impact. A set of log frames and "core evaluation questions" provided an overall conceptual framework for guiding the analysis of the thematic studies. Though the thematic studies drew on a broader range of literature and worldwide data on CDF principles, they were also developed with an explicit objective of ensuring complementarity with the country case studies. The thematic and cross-country studies were undertaken by multidisciplinary teams composed of researchers and evaluators from developed and developing countries.

How Thematic Studies Were Conducted
The four thematic studies were developed in two phases.

■ In the first phase, the thematic papers were developed as desk studies, with most of the analysis focused on donors and other development agencies, especially in terms of assessing the extent to which their behavior—policies, procedures, and practices—has changed sufficiently to enable the implementation of CDF principles to make an impact at the country level. This ensured that the analysis addressed the issues related to quality of development aid—not just in terms of development partnership, but also with regard to the potential influences of the quality of aid on the aid-receiving countries' ability to implement the other three CDF principles.

■ Donor survey questionnaires were constructed by three of the four thematic study

Table A5-1. Bilateral and Multilateral Donor Respondents in Five CDF Case Study Countries

Bilateral donors	CDF case study countries				
	Bolivia	Ghana	Romania	Uganda	Vietnam
Australia - AusAID					●
Belgium					●
Canada - CIDA		●	●		●
Denmark - DANIDA	●	●	●	●	●
Finland					●
France – AFD		●			
Germany - GTZ	●	●	●	●	●*
Ireland				●	
Japan – JBIC & JICA	●	●	●		●*
Netherlands	●	●		●	
New Zealand					●
Ministry of Foreign Affairs, Norway					●
Spain	●				●
Sweden - SIDA	●			●	●
Switzerland - SDC	●		●		●
United Kingdom - DfID	●	●			
United States - USAID		●	●	●	●
(Anonymous)					●*
Multilateral donors					
Asian Development Bank (ADB)					●
European Bank for Reconstruction and Development (EBRD)			●		
European Commission (EC)	●	●	●		●
Inter-American Development Bank (IADB)	●				
International Monetary Fund (IMF)					●
The World Bank (WB)		●	●	●	●
United Nations Children Fund (UNICEF)	●	●	●		●
United Nations Development Programme (UNDP)	●	●	●	●	
United Nations Food and Agriculture Organization (FAO)		●			

Note: ●* = response of two agencies from one country (for example, from both JBIC & JICA).

teams and provided to donor members of the evaluation Steering Committee, who requested their respective operational staffs to respond. The results were incorporated in the report of each study. The draft reports for the first phase were posted on the CDF Evaluation Web site and shared with country case study teams.

- In the second phase, the focus of the analysis was expanded to examine issues related to country-specific aspects of the CDF, where the country case study experiences were used to supplement and enrich the first-phase reports.

Methodology of the Cross-Country Econometric Study

The foci of the cross-country study were twofold: (a) assess the functionality of the ways in which the four CDF principles are being implemented; and (b) assess their potential influence on development impacts. In this context, two sets of analytical approaches were pursued.

Short-term impact of the CDF. The CDF Secretariat survey data on implementation for 46 CDF and PRSP countries (collected in March and July 2001) were used to assess the short-run impact of the CDF on processes and development outcomes. Unfortunately, the very short span of time between the two surveys precluded dynamic analysis of the CDF implementation. However, because of the relatively diverse initial conditions of the 46 countries, even the analysis of the short-term data suggests important policy lessons.

Indicators of the CDF-like Principles
The following section provides further information on the conceptual, data, and methodology

issues related to the construction of proxy indicators for the CDF-like principles.

The indicators of CDF-like principles attempt to approximate the range of development processes envisaged under each CDF principle, using available global databases.[59] The key features of these indicators are informally described in Chapter 3. A more formal exposition follows.

CDF-like Long-Term Holistic (LTH)

The CDF-like long-term holistic indicator is given by the degree of dispersion in CPIA ratings across three broad sectors: Economic Management, Structural Policies, and Policies for Social Inclusion/Equity; and is given by the coefficient of variation (CV):

$$LTH = \frac{\sqrt{\sum_{1}^{n}\left(x_i - \frac{\sum x_i}{n}\right)^2}}{(n-1)\frac{\sum x_i}{n}}, i = 1,2,3$$

where X_i is the rating for the CPIA component i. The CV_k for country K is transformed into a CDF-like long-term holistic index (LTH_k), using the following formula:

$$LTH_k = \frac{Max(CV) - CV_k}{Max(CV) - Min(CV)} \times 100\%$$

where max(CV) and min (CV) are taken for the entire sample across countries. Note that this index falls between 0 and 100. A greater degree of dispersion would suggest less coherence in the country's long-term, holistic development framework.

CDF-like country ownership (OWP): According to the Polity IV codebook, the indicators are defined in the following way: [60]

- Regulation of participation (RP): Participation is regulated to the extent that there are binding rules on when, whether, and how political preferences are expressed. One-party states and Western democracies both regulate participation, but they do so in different ways, the former by channeling participation through a single party structure, with sharp limits on diversity of opinion; the latter by allowing relatively stable and enduring groups to compete nonviolently for political influence. The polar opposite is unregulated participation, in which there are no enduring national political organizations and no effective regime controls on political activity. In such situations, political competition is fluid and often characterized by recurring coercion among shifting coalitions of partisan groups (Marshall and Jaggers 2000, pp. 22-23). A five-category scale is used to code this variable, which ranges from 1 (unregulated) to 5 (regulated).

- Competitiveness of executive recruitment (CER): Competitiveness refers to the extent that prevailing modes of advancement give subordinates equal opportunities to become super-ordinates (Gurr 1974, p. 1483). For example, selection of chief executives through popular elections matching two or more viable parties or candidates is regarded as competitive (Marshall and Jaggers 2000). A three-category measure is used: 1 (selection) to 3 (election).

- Openness of executive recruitment (OER): Recruitment of the chief executive is "open" to the extent that all the politically active population has an opportunity, in principle, to attain the position through a regularized process. In considering recruitment, it must first be determined whether there are any established modes at all by which chief executives are selected.

Regulation refers to the extent to which a polity has institutionalized procedures for transferring executive power (Gurr 1974). A four-category measure is used, ranging from 1(closed) to 4(open).

- Constraints on chief executive (CCE): This variable refers to the extent of institutionalized constraints on the decisionmaking powers of chief executives, whether individuals or collectivities. Such limitations may be imposed by any "accountability groups." In Western democracies these are usually legislatures. Other kinds of accountability groups are the ruling party in a one-party state; councils of nobles or powerful advisors in monarchies; the military in coup-prone polities; and in many states, a strong, independent judiciary. The concern is therefore with the checks and balances among these groups (Gurr 1974). A seven-category scale is used, ranging from 1 (unlimited authority) to 7 (executive parity or subordination).

The CDF-like country ownership index (OWP) is a simple average:

$OWP= 1/4(RP+CER+OER+CCE)$, where it is scaled to be between 0 and 100, using the following transformation:

$$\frac{OWP - min(OWP)}{Max(OWP) - Min(OWP)} \ x \ 100\%$$

CDF-like Country-led Partnership (PA): This is represented by the average of "excessive" technical assistance and the ratio of concentration of donors in the recipient country to how aid is distributed across different sectors in the economy of the country. A high ratio suggests either high donor concentration, and hence less difficulty in achieving coordination among donors; low sectoral concentration of aid, which means that aid is more evenly distributed across sectors, and hence the aid regime is likely to promote holistic development; or both.

(a) Donor Fragmentation (HHI$_D$): measured by a Herfindahl-Hirschman Index, which is a simple, yet sophisticated, way of measuring donor fragmentation/concentration. Squaring the share of each donor's share as a percentage of bilateral aid and then summing those squares obtains the Herfindahl-Hirschman Index. The Herfindahl-Hirschman Index helps differentiate between one country in which four donors contribute equal amounts of bilateral aid, and another where one donor contributes a 70 percent share, and three others, 10 percent each. The former, which is more fragmented, would have a lower Herfindahl-Hirschman Index.

(b) Sectoral Concentration of Aid (HHI$_s$): is the Herfendal-Hirchman Index on sectoral allocation of foreign assistance, which measures the concentration of aid (ODA) across five major sectors: social infrastructure and services; economic infrastructure; production sectors; multi-sector and commodity aid; and general program assistance.

(c) "Excessive" technical assistance: is calculated by taking the deviation of the share of technical assistance in total aid a country receives (T) from the "optimal" technical assistance for that country (T^*). That is, excessive technical assistance is given by:

$\frac{T}{T^*}$, where T^* for country i is derived from the following expression:

$$I_{it} = a_0 + a_1 T_{it\text{-}1} + a_2 T_{t\text{-}1} \times I_{it\text{-}2} - a_3 T_{it\text{-}1}^2 \times I_{it\text{-}2} + \beta_0 x_0 ,$$

where a's are the coefficients,[61] T is actual technical assistance, and I is the a measure of institutional capacity in country i and is given by the *ICRG* variable taken from the International Country Risk data base.[62] X is the initial conditions. The underlying assumption in the above specification is that technical assistance improves institutional capacity (the positive coefficient of T), though its effect is subject to diminishing returns (the negative coefficient of T^2). Moreover, the specification suggests that countries with poor initial institutions stand to gain more by receiving technical assistance (the negative coefficient of the $T x I$ term).

Table A5-1. Descriptive Statistics of the CDF-like Variable and Its Components, 1980-2000

CDF-like	Mean	Median	Std deviation	Min	Max
Long-term holistic	63	67	17	16	100
Country ownership	46	43	29	00	100
Country-led partnership	55	55	11	21(16)	86
Results orientation	54	55	16	14	88
Overall CDF-like	55	54	12	24	82

Note: See notes to figure 3.1. The individual countries included in the table are—Sub-Saharan Africa: Angola, Benin, Burkina Faso, Burundi, Cameroon, Cape Verde, Central African Republic, Chad, Comoros, Ethiopia, Gabon, Gambia, Ghana, Guinea, Kenya, Mauritania, Mauritius, Mozambique, Senegal, Seychelles, Swaziland, Tanzania, Togo, Uganda, Zambia, Zimbabwe; Middle East and North Africa: Algeria, Egypt, Jordan, Morocco, Tunisia, Turkey, Yemen; Latin America and Caribbean: Belize, Bolivia, Brazil, Chile, Colombia, Dominican Republic, Ecuador, El Salvador, Grenada, Guatemala, Guyana, Haiti, Honduras, Jamaica, Panama, Paraguay, Peru, St. Lucia, St. Vincent, Trinidad and Tobago, Uruguay, Venezuela; East Asia: China, Fiji, Indonesia, Korea, Rep., Philippines, Thailand, Vietnam; South Asia: Bangladesh, India, Nepal, Pakistan, Sri Lanka.

Table A5-2. Distribution of CDF-like Principles

Score	Long-term holistic	Country ownership	Country-led partnership	Results orientation	Overall CDF-like
0-20	2	27	0	3	0
20-40	8	26	12	16	15
40-60	29	21	68	46	56
60-80	56	21	31	45	40
80-100	17	17	1	2	1

Note: The data are averages for the period 1980-2000.

The optimum level of technical assistance (T^*), which maximizes institutional capacity (I), is, therefore, given by

$$T_{it}^* = \frac{a_1 + a_2 I_{it-2}}{2a_3 I_{it-2}} \ .$$

The optimal level of technical assistance varies with a country's level of institutions. The regression estimate of the above equation provides the values of the parameters that define the above expression (see Elbadawi, Mavrotas, and Randa 2003 for further details).

Finally, the quality of aid index is given as a simple average of the concentration ratio and an "inverse" measure of "excessive" technical assistance:

$$PA = (1/2) \left[\left(\frac{T^*}{T}\right) + \left(\frac{HHI_D}{HHI_s}\right) \right] ,$$

where it is scaled to be between 0 and 100, using the following transformation:

$$\frac{PA - min(PA)}{Max(PA) - Min(PA)} \ x \ 100\% \ .$$

CDF-like Results Orientation (RO)

The indicator for results orientation is the rating given to question 15 of the Country Policy and Institutional Assessment (CPIA) that asks for an assessment of poverty monitoring and analysis. As previously, the RO is normalized.

This index means that one of the four CDF-like principles that make up the overall CDF-like index is a component of the CPIA. This, however, should not pose a serious problem for subsequent regressions where both CDF-like and CPIA indexes are included, since this sub-index is only one of 20 components of CPIA; it accounts only for 9 of the weight (see below the expression for the overall CDF-like index). Finally, all regression results remain unchanged when using an overall CDF-like index without including the CPIA component.

Overall CDF-like

The overall *CDF-like* score is a simple average of the four principles, subscribing to the central concept of CDF that regards all principles as equally important for a CDF approach to development. Therefore,

CDF-like=1/4[LTH+ OWP+PA+RO].

Some Summary Statistics

Summary statistics for the five CDF-like indexes for 88 countries spanning the 1980-2000 period are described in table A5-1.

Table A5-2 presents the distribution of the CDF-like principles for the 88 countries over the 1980-2000 period. It is notable that the index of overall CDF-like principles (which will be the only index subsequently used in the empirical analysis) has an approximate bell-shaped distribution.

Analysis based on CDF-like Principles. Although the CDF, as an explicit initiative, was introduced in 1999, its principles were previously practiced at various times in different countries. Therefore, an index of CDF-like principles was developed and combined with global cross-country data to estimate the marginal contribution of the implementation of CDF-like development strategies to development outcomes. The index of CDF-like principles was constructed to capture:

- CDF-like long-term holistic principle: measured by optimum investment gap

- CDF-like country ownership principle: measured by participation and contestability components of Polity IV

- CDF-like country-led partnership principle: measured by quality of aid

- CDF-like results orientation principle: measured by the CPIA sub-indicator of poverty-tracking capacity.

The proxy indicators of CDF-like principles were derived from 88 countries for the period 1980-2000. Similar to the numerical CDF indexes, the indexes of CDF-like principles were normalized to fall between 0 and 100, and the overall CDF-like index was obtained by using the statistical technique of "principal components." A detailed discussion of the cross-country econometric approach and findings is found in Elbadawi, Mavrotas, and Randa 2002, "Development Impact of CDF-Like Strategies," a thematic background paper to this evaluation. The paper is available upon request.

Business Environment Indicators and CDF-like Strategy Index

Patterns of Association

Figures A5-1–A5-4 show CDF-like indices for countries plotted against four indicators of the business environment: contract enforcement, credit markets, private sector entry regulations, and labor regulations. The discussion of business environment and the CDF in Chapter 3 draws on these figures.

Figure A5-1. CDF and Contract Enforcement

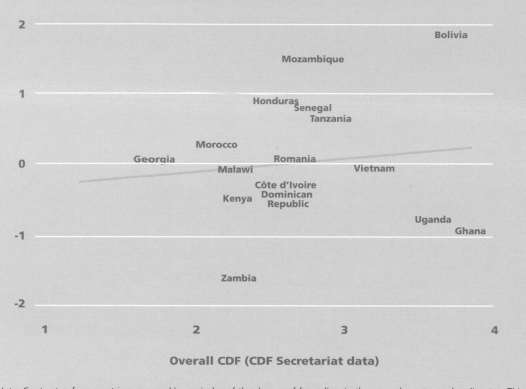

Overall CDF (CDF Secretariat data)

Note: Contract enforcement is measured by an index of the degree of formalism in the procedures to resolve disputes. This index measures substantive and procedural statutory intervention in judicial cases at lower-level civil trial courts. It includes, among other measures: whether the resolution of the case provided would rely mostly on the intervention of professional judges and attorneys, as opposed to the intervention of other types of adjudicators and lay people; the level of legal justification required in the process of dispute resolution, and the formalities required to engage someone in the procedure or to hold him/her accountable for the judgment. The index ranges from 0 (weak contract enforcement) to 7 (superior contract enforcement).

Figure A5-2. CDF and Credit Market for the Private Sector

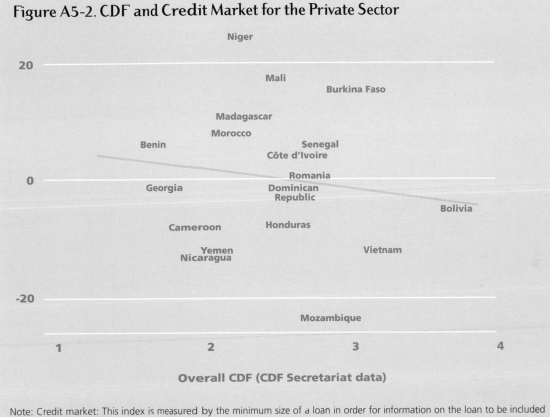

Overall CDF (CDF Secretariat data)

Note: Credit market: This index is measured by the minimum size of a loan in order for information on the loan to be included in the Public Credit Registries, divided by GNI per capita. The data are objective, so there is no range given. However, higher values indicate that credit histories of large borrowers are the ones that are available, and small borrowers do not have a chance of building their credit history. That is – low values (environment good for both small and big business) – high values (environment good only for big business).

Figure A5-3. CDF and Private Sector Entry Regulations

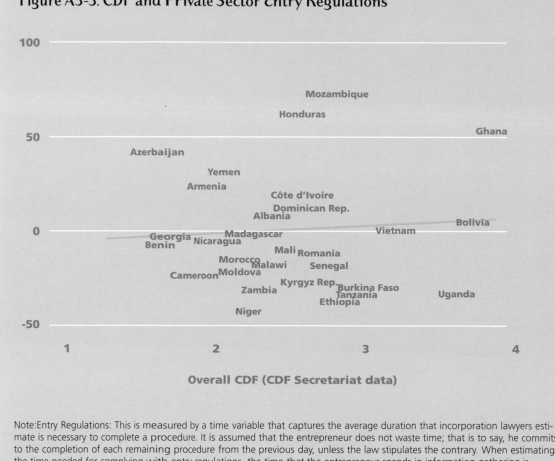

Overall CDF (CDF Secretariat data)

Note:Entry Regulations: This is measured by a time variable that captures the average duration that incorporation lawyers esti-mate is necessary to complete a procedure. It is assumed that the entrepreneur does not waste time; that is to say, he commits to the completion of each remaining procedure from the previous day, unless the law stipulates the contrary. When estimating the time needed for complying with entry regulations, the time that the entrepreneur spends in information gathering is ignored. The entrepreneur is aware of all entry regulations and their sequence from the very beginning. This is objective data—higher values discourage the entry of new firms into an industry. Lower values indicate easy entry of new firms.

Figure A5-4. CDF and Labor Regulation

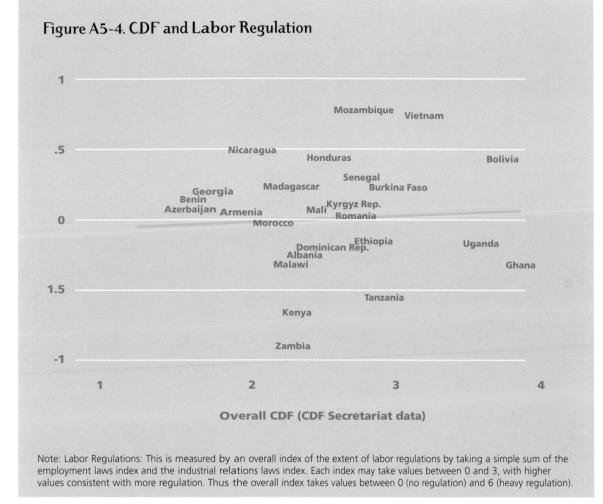

Overall CDF (CDF Secretariat data)

Note: Labor Regulations: This is measured by an overall index of the extent of labor regulations by taking a simple sum of the employment laws index and the industrial relations laws index. Each index may take values between 0 and 3, with higher values consistent with more regulation. Thus the overall index takes values between 0 (no regulation) and 6 (heavy regulation).

Evaluation Survey Instruments

This annex reproduces the two survey instruments used for the six country case studies and four thematic studies.

A) Government-Donor Relations: Changes and Trends

As a specific parallel exercise to the five CDF pilot case study countries (Bolivia, Ghana, Romania, Uganda, Vietnam), a questionnaire survey instrument was developed to capture facts and figures on the current status and trends in relations between government and development partners. Specifically, the survey attempts to identify the impact on governments of donor procedural requirements, and the transaction costs they imply.

A. Composition of portfolio
Please tell us about the activities that your agency is responsible for in Ghana.

a1: Approximately how many projects, including "non-project" or programmatic assistance operations, does your agency currently have in your approved portfolio for Ghana? Please check the applicable range.

❑ < 5   ❑ 5-10   ❑ 10-20   ❑ 20-40   ❑ >40   If available, what is the exact number? _____

a2: Has the average size of such operations decreased or increased over the last 5 years? Please check the applicable range.

❑ Increased   ❑ Remained the same   ❑ Decreased

a3: How many, if any, of your agency's project and programme operations in Ghana are part of wider funding schemes where other donors are also contributing (in joint sector-wide programmes [SWAps], as cofinancing, or in other modalities)? Please check the applicable range.

❑ < 3   ❑ 3-5   ❑ 5-10   ❑ 10-20   ❑ >20   If available, what is the exact number?_____

a4: What approximate share of your agency's total annual disbursements over your last two fiscal years is accounted for by jointly funded project and programme operations in Ghana? Please check applicable range.

❑ <20%   ❑ 20-40%   ❑ 40-60%   ❑ 60-80%   ❑ >80%

a5. Has this share increased over the last 5 years?   ❑ Yes   ❑ No

a6. Please add possible other comments regarding trends of change in the portfolio of your agency in Ghana.

B. Coordination with other donors

Please give us your (and your colleagues') assessments of the efficiency and effectiveness of donor coordination activities.

b1: In your perception, has there been a change in the frequency of donor coordination activities in which your agency has been involved during the last five years? Please check the applicable range and elaborate.

   ❑ Increased   ❑ Remained the same   ❑ Decreased

b2: In which coordination activities of a recurring nature that deal with donor assistance *as a whole* does your agency participate?

   ❑ Consultative Group (CG) Meetings
   ❑ Mini-CG Meetings
   ❑ Other (please specify nature of meeting, frequency, and whether Government is invited)

b3: In which coordination activities dealing with *specific* sector or project issues and involving other donors does your agency participate? In each category below, please specify sector, frequency of meetings, and whether Government is invited.

   (1) Sector Issues
   (2) Project Issues
   (3) Other

b4: In your perception (and those of your colleagues), has

   (1) the efficiency of donor coordination improved, deteriorated or remained the same over the last five years?

   ❑ Deteriorated   ❑ Remained the same   ❑ Improved

   (2) Is donor coordination efficiency currently satisfactory in your view?   ❑ Yes   ❑ No

   (3) Have the results (effectiveness) of donor coordination improved, deteriorated or remained the same over the last five years?

   ❑ Deteriorated   ❑ Remained the same   ❑ Improved

   (4) Are they currently satisfactory in your view?   ❑ Yes   ❑ No

   (5) What specific means could improve efficiency and effectiveness? Please specify.

b5. (1) In your view, are there instances where *country*-led aid coordination is or was particularly efficient and/or effective? Please specify.

(2) In your view, are there instances where country-led aid coordination is or was particularly *inefficient* and/or *ineffective*? Please specify.

(3) In your view, have there been instances where *donor*-led aid coordination is or was more efficient and/or effective than country-led aid coordination? Please specify.

b6: What in your view have been the key achievements of coordination activities, if any, over the last 5 years? Please check all that apply and provide examples wherever possible.

❏ Increased selectivity among donors so as to avoid overlap
❏ Better alignment of approaches and with Ghanaian strategy/GPRS
❏ More efficient policy dialogue
❏ Adoption of common procedures, such as joint missions, reports, procurement, or budget and disbursement cycles?
❏ Others (please specify)

b7. Please add possible other comments regarding trends in aid coordination in Ghana.

C. Donor administrative and procedural requirements
Please tell us about your agency's administrative and procedural requirements.

c1. (1) How many preparation/appraisal missions (or visits) have staff and/or consultants from your agency's headquarters undertaken to Ghana in the last 12 months?
   ❏ < 3   ❏ 3-5   ❏ 5-10   ❏ >10   If available, what is the exact number?_____

(2) How many of these have been undertaken jointly with other donors?
   ❏ < 3   ❏ 3-5   ❏ 5-10   ❏ >10   If available, what is the exact number?_____

(3) Over the last 5 years, has the number of joint preparation/appraisal missions
   ❏ Increased   ❏ Remained the same   ❏ Decreased

c2. (1) How many monitoring and evaluation missions have staff and/or consultants from your agency's headquarters undertaken to Ghana in the last 12 months?
   ❏ < 3   ❏ 3-5   ❏ 5-10   ❏ >10   If available, what is the exact number?_____

(2) How many of these have been undertaken jointly with other donors?
   ❏ < 3   ❏ 3-5   ❏ 5-10   ❏ >10   If available, what is the exact number?_____

(3) Over the last 5 years, has the number of joint monitoring and evaluation missions
   ❏ Increased   ❏ Remained the same   ❏ Decreased

c3. How many reports (progress and financial) does your agency normally require from Government per year for:

    (1) projects? ❑ 1   ❑ 2   ❑ 4   ❑ Other:____

    (2) non-project assistance or budget support? ❑ 1   ❑ 2   ❑ 4   ❑ Other:____

    (3) Over the last five years, has the number of reports required:
    ❑ Increased   ❑ Remained the same   ❑ Decreased

c4. (1) Has your agency ever adopted a joint reporting format endorsed or prepared by the government? ❑ Yes   ❑ No
    If yes, in how many cases? ❑ < 3   ❑ 3-5   ❑ 5-10   ❑ >10

    (2) What has been the trend, if any, over the last 5 years, in the use of joint formats?
    ❑ Increased   ❑ Remained the same   ❑ Decreased

c5. For Ghana projects and programmes (non-project operations), has your agency adopted:

    (1) the procurement rules of other agencies? ❑ Yes   ❑ No
    If yes, in how many cases? ❑ < 3   ❑ 3-5   ❑ 5-10   ❑ >10

    (2) government procurement procedures? ❑ Yes   ❑ No
    If yes, in how many cases? ❑ < 3   ❑ 3-5   ❑ 5-10   ❑ >10

    (3) What have been the trends, if any, in each category over the last 5 years?
    Procurement rules of other agencies: ❑ Increased   ❑ Remained the same   ❑ Decreased

    Government procurement rules: ❑ Increased   ❑ Remained the same   ❑ Decreased

c6. In your view, how has the move from project aid to various types of programme aid affected:

    (1) the amount of negotiation and meeting time before and during preparation?
    ❑ Increased   ❑ Remained the same   ❑ Decreased

    (2) the amount of paperwork?
    ❑ Increased   ❑ Remained the same   ❑ Decreased

    (3) Please give examples if possible:

c7: Please add possible other comments regarding trends in and impact of donor procedural requirements in Ghana.

D. Implementation practices

The questions in the next two sections deal with donor practices.

d1. Does your agency offer salary incentives (topping up, sitting allowances, consultancy contracts to civil servants, per diem etc.) to national staff (regular staff and local consultants) involved in implementation of project or programmes your agency funds in Ghana?   ❏ Yes   ❏ No

If yes, (1) In how many of the projects and programmes funded by your agency are such incentives offered?

❏ <20%   ❏ 20-40%   ❏ 40-60%   ❏ 60-80%   ❏ >80%

(2) Why does your agency find it necessary to provide these additional incentives? Please specify:

(3) In the last 5 years, have the amount of such incentives

❏ Increased   ❏ Remained the same   ❏ Decreased

d.2 Does your agency use project or programme implementation or management units in Ghana?
❏ Yes   ❏ No

If yes, (1) How many are currently active?

❏ < 3   ❏ 3-5   ❏ 5-10   ❏ >10

(2) Please explain the main reasons for using such units.

(3) Does you agency plan to continue using such units as they exist today in the foreseeable future?   ❏ Yes   ❏ No

(4) What are your plans for their future use?

d3. To what extent does "disbursement pressure"—the explicit or implicit requirement in your agency's policy that assigned funds must be spent in the budget year or over a given period– influence your agency's choice of the above or other implementation practices? Please give specific examples.

d4. Does your agency use special measures, such as fiduciary, environmental and social safeguards, on top of the government's own management & control system?   ❏ Yes   ❏ No

If yes, (1) Please specify which measures you use.

(2) Why does your agency find such measures necessary?

d5. (1) How much of your agency's assistance to Ghana is tied to procurement of goods and services, including TA, in your own country?

❏ <20%   ❏ 20-40%   ❏ 40-60%   ❏ 60-80%   ❏ >80%

(2) In the last 5 years, has this share

❏ Increased   ❏ Remained the same   ❏ Decreased

(3) Does your agency in Ghana have any discretion over source of procurement, or is this determined by your headquarters?

d6. Which approximate share of your agency's annual disbursement in Ghana is used on:

(1) internationally recruited TA?

❏ <20%   ❏ 20-40%   ❏ 40-60%   ❏ 60-80%   ❏ >80%

(2) locally recruited TA?

❏ <20%   ❏ 20-40%   ❏ 40-60%   ❏ 60-80%   ❏ >80%

(3) What have been the trends over the last 5 years?

Total amount of TA: ❏ Increased   ❏ Remained the same   ❏ Decreased

Internationally recruited TA: ❏ Increased   ❏ Remained the same   ❏ Decreased

Locally recruited TA: ❏ Increased   ❏ Remained the same   ❏ Decreased

d7. (1) How often does your agency report on planned and actual expenditures to the Government of Ghana?

❏ Annually   ❏ Bi-annually   ❏ Quarterly   ❏ Other:_____

(2) Has the frequency of reporting over the last 5 years

❏ Increased   ❏ Remained the same   ❏ Decreased

d8. Do you (and your colleagues) consider the information that your agency provides to the Ghanaian government timely and sufficient, and in principle enabling the government to include your agency's assistance in the national budget and accounts?   ❏ Yes   ❏ No
Please explain.

d9. Please add possible other comments regarding implementation practices.

B) Government-Donor Relations: Changes and Trends

As a specific parallel exercise to the four thematic studies (Long-term Holistic Framework, Country Ownership, Country-led Partnership, and Results Orientation), a structured survey questionnaire instrument was developed to assess the extent of implementation of the four CDF principles by development partners. The survey was administered to bilateral and multilateral donors both at headquarters and in country offices.

Long-term Holistic Frameworks

1) Our organization has endorsed the principle of Long-term Holistic Framework as essential to development cooperation: ❑ -2 ❑ -1 ❑ 0 ❑ +1 ❑ +2 ❑ ?

2) Our *government* has decided that bilateral aid shall preferably be based on longer-term financial frameworks. ❑ -2 ❑ -1 ❑ 0 ❑ +1 ❑ +2 ❑ ?

3) *Parliamentary debates/decisions* on development co-operation support linking resources to longer-term framework agreements with partner countries.
❑ -2 ❑ -1 ❑ 0 ❑ +1 ❑ +2 ❑ ?

4) Our direct bilateral agreements with partner countries are increasingly based on longer-term framework arrangements (strategies, memoranda of understanding).
❑ -2 ❑ -1 ❑ 0 ❑ +1 ❑ +2 ❑ ?

5) The average time horizon for our country's bilateral agreements (project, programs, country strategies) is longer now than they were three years ago.
❑ -2 ❑ -1 ❑ 0 ❑ +1 ❑ +2 ❑ ?

6) Our organisation/government is now allocating a higher *share* of bilateral aid to longer-term framework agreements (macro/budget or sector support, SWAPs).
❑ -2 ❑ -1 ❑ 0 ❑ +1 ❑ +2 ❑ ?

   If the answer was a "+1" or "+2," please explain/specify:

7) Our partner countries see us as being a more predictable donor in terms of structure and commitment of financial flows. ❑ -2 ❑ -1 ❑ 0 ❑ +1 ❑ +2 ❑ ?

8) We are systematically building our capacity for our own long-term holistic planning.
❑ -2 ❑ -1 ❑ 0 ❑ +1 ❑ +2 ❑ ?

9) We have developed new instruments that strengthen our ability to carry out long-term holistic planning. ❑ -2 ❑ -1 ❑ 0 ❑ +1 ❑ +2 ❑ ?

   If the answer was a "+1" or "+2," please explain/specify:

10) Our staff training is now focusing more on program approaches and less on project management. ❏ -2   ❏ -1   ❏ 0   ❏ +1   ❏ +2   ❏ ?

11) We are increasing our capacity to discuss, analyse and contribute to partners' longer-term planning instruments and processes (PERs, SWAPs, etc.) (putting more staff in the field, hiring more strategy/macro and fewer project staff, etc)   ❏ -2   ❏ -1   ❏ 0   ❏ +1   ❏ +2   ❏ ?

If the answer was a "+1" or "+2," please explain/specify:

12) Our organisation considers LTHF as important a concept in our dialogue with our partners as ownership and country-led partnership.   ❏ -2   ❏ -1   ❏ 0   ❏ +1   ❏ +2   ❏ ?

13) LTHF is discussed as a key concept in international donor co-ordination meetings (DAC meetings, SPA meetings).   ❏ -2   ❏ -1   ❏ 0   ❏ +1   ❏ +2   ❏ ?

14) LTHF is discussed as an important concept in in-country donor meetings.
❏ -2   ❏ -1   ❏ 0   ❏ +1   ❏ +2   ❏ ?

15) LTHF is increasingly discussed as an important concept with partner country governments.
❏ -2   ❏ -1   ❏ 0   ❏ +1   ❏ +2   ❏ ?

B. Donors' Views on LTHF in Partner Countries

16) Partner countries' *understanding* of LTHF is clear.   ❏ -2   ❏ -1   ❏ 0   ❏ +1   ❏ +2   ❏ ?

17) Partner countries' *embrace* of LTHF is more rhetoric than reality.
❏ -2   ❏ -1   ❏ 0   ❏ +1   ❏ +2   ❏ ?

18) We see that there is an increasing interest and political will in the partner countries to move toward LTHF approaches   ❏ -2   ❏ -1   ❏ 0   ❏ +1   ❏ +2   ❏ ?

19) If LTHF has not been adopted in some countries, it is due to lack of political will
❏ -2   ❏ -1   ❏ 0   ❏ +1   ❏ +2   ❏ ?

20) If LTHF has not been adopted in some countries, it is due to lack of internal planning capacity
❏ -2   ❏ -1   ❏ 0   ❏ +1   ❏ +2   ❏ ?

21) If donors had wanted partner countries to adopt LTHF faster/more consistently, they could have provided more political and capacity building support   ❏ -2   ❏ -1   ❏ 0   ❏ +1   ❏ +2   ❏ ?

22) The donor community has been consistent and constructive in its dialogue with partner countries on the need to adopt and implement LTHF approaches
❏ -2   ❏ -1   ❏ 0   ❏ +1   ❏ +2   ❏ ?

23) Some partner countries see LTHF as another donor-imposed concept that they are highly sceptical to. ❑ -2   ❑ -1   ❑ 0   ❑ +1   ❑ +2   ❑ ?

24) Some partner countries see the LTHF as too sophisticated and demanding for their own political and administrative structures to be able to cope with
❑ -2   ❑ -1   ❑ 0   ❑ +1   ❑ +2   ❑ ?

25) In partner countries that have in principle adopted an LTHF approach, this is reflected in the following changes over the last three years:

They are now producing better quality *long-term vision documents*.
❑ -2   ❑ -1   ❑ 0   ❑ +1   ❑ +2   ❑ ?

There are better economic/financial *links and consistency* between long-term vision documents, medium term frames (MTEFs, PRSPs) and annual budgets and plans
❑ -2   ❑ -1   ❑ 0   ❑ +1   ❑ +2   ❑ ?

There is better balance between *sectors*   ❑ -2   ❑ -1   ❑ 0   ❑ +1   ❑ +2   ❑ ?

There is better balance between *economic/financial* and *human/structural/social* dimensions
❑ -2   ❑ -1   ❑ 0   ❑ +1   ❑ +2   ❑ ?

Programming/planning *within* sectors is now better (SWAPs, sector programs)
❑ -2   ❑ -1   ❑ 0   ❑ +1   ❑ +2   ❑ ?

26) We see that countries that are CDF pilots have been better at moving toward LTHF than non-CDF partner countries.   ❑ -2   ❑ -1   ❑ 0   ❑ +1   ❑ +2   ❑ ?

Comments:

C. Donors' Support for LTHF in Partner Countries

27) We support partner countries that ask assistance for preparing larger frameworks for our assistance (sector programs, macro planning).   ❑ -2   ❑ -1   ❑ 0   ❑ +1   ❑ +2   ❑ ?

28) We now provide more assistance to activities that contribute to longer-term and more holistic planning (planning entities/activities in ministries of planning, line ministries where we provide assistance).   ❑ -2   ❑ -1   ❑ 0   ❑ +1   ❑ +2   ❑ ?

29) We use own staff time to support the development of LTHF-like processes in the field (SWAPs, PRSPs).   ❑ -2   ❑ -1   ❑ 0   ❑ +1   ❑ +2   ❑ ?

30) Our organisation now demands that partner countries provide larger frameworks as part of the request for assistance.   ❑ -2   ❑ -1   ❑ 0   ❑ +1   ❑ +2   ❑ ?

Comments:

D. LTHF Instruments

31) The basic LTHF instrumentarium in a country should be the country's own budget and planning instruments. ❑ -2   ❑ -1   ❑ 0   ❑ +1   ❑ +2   ❑ ?

32) A matrix was proposed as a basis for a holistic framework in Mr. Wolfensohn's January 1999 launching of the CDF.

We see this matrix as a useful tool for holistic planning.
❑ -2   ❑ -1   ❑ 0   ❑ +1   ❑ +2   ❑ ?

We see this matrix as useful for analysing where donors should allocate their resources
❑ -2   ❑ -1   ❑ 0   ❑ +1   ❑ +2   ❑ ?

We see the matrix more as a heuristic/pedagogical way of talking about holistic planning rather than as a concrete planning tool/instrument.
❑ -2   ❑ -1   ❑ 0   ❑ +1   ❑ +2   ❑ ?

We use this matrix approach to verify if a partner's planning can be considered holistic.
❑ -2   ❑ -1   ❑ 0   ❑ +1   ❑ +2   ❑ ?

We have never seen the matrix used by any partner country's authorities.
❑ -2   ❑ -1   ❑ 0   ❑ +1   ❑ +2   ❑ ?

33) Later in 1999, the Poverty Reduction Strategy Paper (PRSP) was launched:

We see PRSPs as the best current instrument for LTHF.
❑ -2   ❑ -1   ❑ 0   ❑ +1   ❑ +2   ❑ ?

We see current PRSPs as a step in the right direction toward LTHF.
❑ -2   ❑ -1   ❑ 0   ❑ +1   ❑ +2   ❑ ?

We see the PRSPs as being too limited in terms of sectors/issues (not holistic enough).
❑ -2   ❑ -1   ❑ 0   ❑ +1   ❑ +2   ❑ ?

We see the PRSPs as being too short-term (3 year delivery horizon - not long-term enough).
❑ -2   ❑ -1   ❑ 0   ❑ +1   ❑ +2   ❑ ?

Comments:

34) The Millennium Development Goals (MDGs) are now the basic set of goals that development assistance/ efforts are to work toward.

We see the MDGs as sufficiently long-term but not holistic enough.
❑ -2   ❑ -1   ❑ 0   ❑ +1   ❑ +2   ❑ ?

We see the MDGs as encompassing the key areas and thus for most countries being sufficiently holistic. ❑ -2   ❑ -1   ❑ 0   ❑ +1   ❑ +2   ❑ ?

35) Please rank the following instruments for LTHF in order of importance, "1" most important, "5" least:

_____ The CDF Matrix
_____ PRSPs
_____ MDGs
_____ Sector plans (SWAPs etc)
_ National planning/budget documents that require Parliamentary approval

Comments:

E. Factors that Facilitated the Move toward LTHF

36) The trend seems to be toward LTHF in partner countries. Please rank the following factors in order of importance, "1" most important, "5" least:

_____ Internal developments in partner countries
_____ The launching of OECD's "Shaping the 21st Century"
_____ The launching of the CDF
_____ The launching of the PRSP
_____ The general international trend as reflected in the International Conferences with focus on overarching/long-term holistic goals

37) The CDF is seen as contributing toward LTHF. Please rank the following factors in order of importance, "1" most important, "5" least:

_____ The CDF presented an original articulation of LTHF
_____ The CDF was more focused, operational on the need for LTHF
_____ The CDF was launched by the Bank, Mr. Wolfensohn
_____ The Bank has put considerable resources behind the CDF
_____ The CDF reinforced/strengthened widely accepted but not well implemented principles

F. LTHF and Impact on Results

38) We see that partner countries that use LTHF are more efficient users of own limited planning and co-ordination resources. ❑ -2   ❑ -1   ❑ 0   ❑ +1   ❑ +2   ❑ ?

39) We see that governments that use LTHF are more active/more efficient at donor co-ordination. ❑ -2   ❑ -1   ❑ 0   ❑ +1   ❑ +2   ❑ ?

40) One of the gains from using LTHF in the donor-partner dialogue is that it is supposed to reduce various transaction costs.

We see that using LTHF reduces internal planning/co-ordination costs in our partner countries
❑ -2   ❑ -1   ❑ 0   ❑ +1   ❑ +2   ❑ ?

We see that using LTHF reduces aid co-ordination costs between donors and host authorities
❑ -2   ❑ -1   ❑ 0   ❑ +1   ❑ +2   ❑ ?

We see that using LTHF generates gains primarily to the host government.
❑ -2   ❑ -1   ❑ 0   ❑ +1   ❑ +2   ❑ ?

We see that using LTHF generates gains primarily to the donors.
❑ -2   ❑ -1   ❑ 0   ❑ +1   ❑ +2   ❑ ?

Comments:

41) We see that countries that are moving toward LTHF are better able to align their own objectives and resources toward attaining the MDGs.
❑ -2   ❑ -1   ❑ 0   ❑ +1   ❑ +2   ❑ ?

If the answer was a "+1" or "+2," please explain/specify:

42) Indications are that those countries that are using more long-term frameworks are more successful at attaining the MDGs.[63]   ❑ -2   ❑ -1   ❑ 0   ❑ +1   ❑ +2   ❑ ?

Comments:

G. Bottom Line/Summing Up

43) We consider the LTHF as a key concept for more efficient and effective use of development resources.   ❑ -2   ❑ -1   ❑ 0   ❑ +1   ❑ +2   ❑ ?

44) It is our impression that the donor community consider LTHF as a key concept for more efficient and effective use of development resources.   ❑ -2   ❑ -1   ❑ 0   ❑ +1   ❑ +2   ❑ ?

45) It is our impression that our partner countries consider LTHF as a key concept for more efficient and effective use of development resources.   ❑ -2   ❑ -1   ❑ 0   ❑ +1   ❑ +2   ❑ ?

46) It is our impression that use of LTHF approaches is increasing in importance and quality, and that this trend is likely to continue in the years to come.
❑ -2   ❑ -1   ❑ 0   ❑ +1   ❑ +2   ❑ ?

Thank you very much for your time!!

Country Ownership

Please check the appropriate response

Part 0 – General

0.1. Do you feel that the principle of ownership within the CDF has had a significant impact in terms of influencing the design and implementation of your assistance programs?
❑ Yes   ❑ No

0.2. Has your organization aligned its operational policies, procedures and practices to support country ownership?   ❑ Yes   ❑ No

0.3. If yes, please give the date:

0.4. How have these policies evolved since then? (Please elaborate).

0.5. Has the implementation of the CDF principle of greater ownership meant an increased concern for any of the following?
❑ Participation   ❑ Women   ❑ Human rights   ❑ Capacity building   ❑ Other (please specify)

0.6. Has your organization, in support of the ownership principle, increased its support in these areas?   ❑ Yes   ❑ No

0.7 Please elaborate

Part I – Allocation and Prioritization of Aid Flows

Until the mid 1990's, it would seem that most aid recipients did not have a long-term vision to help aid donors align aid allocation with country priorities or such a vision was not home grown.

I.1 Before 1995, did most recipient governments you worked with have a long-term national vision?   ❑ Yes   ❑ No

I.2 When did they start adopting such a vision? Date:

I.3 Has your organization contributed to the formulation of any country's development strategy?
❑ Yes   ❑ No

I.4 If yes, in which sectors have you made a contribution:
❑ Poverty Reduction   ❑ Civil Service Reform   ❑ Governance   ❑ Education
❑ Health   ❑ Overall design of vision   ❑ Other (please specify):

I.5 In the formulation of the country's long and medium term development program, do you accept local priorities in a systematic way?   ❑ Yes   ❑ No

I.6   Do governments publicly disseminate their long-term development goals? ❑ Yes   ❑ No

Donors may feel there is a strong need to support institution building while governments prefer assistance in stone and mortar sectors:

I.7   Rank the following sectors according to your priorities for donor assistance:
       _____ Sectoral (agriculture, finance, manufacturing….).
       _____ Infrastructure (electricity, water, telecommunications…)
       _____ Human Development (health, education, poverty alleviation, SMEs, human rights, good governance…)
       _____ Judiciary system (training of judges, reforming of dispute settlement mechanism…)
       _____ Legislative reform (competition law, labor law…)
       _____ Civil Service reform (transparency, accountability)

I.8   Do you usually impose certain conditions on the borrowing/ recipient country in order to allocate your funds? ❑ Yes   ❑ No

I.9   If yes, what kind of thematic concerns of the project do you insist upon?
       ❑ Gender equality   ❑ Capacity Building   ❑ Social dimensions   ❑ Governance

Aid Performance Monitoring

I.10   Has greater ownership of the country's development program resulted in a changed approach to performance monitoring and evaluation of the aid being disbursed by your organization?
       ❑ Yes   ❑ No

I.11   If yes, in what way?

I.12   Is the information being reported, of the kind and form, that is also useful to the recipient country (e.g. budget preparation and planning) or does it serve your organization's purposes only? ❑ Yes   ❑ No

Part II – Technical Assistance (TA) for Capacity and Institutional Building

TA can be a double-edged sword, since increased allocation toward TA will not necessarily improve local participation and ownership and may be dissipated back to donors.

II.1   Do you feel that the contracting mode of receiving TA affects the ownership outcome of the project? ❑ Yes   ❑ No

II.2   Do you as a donor require the involvement of TA suppliers from designated donor sources?
       ❑ Yes   ❑ No

II.3   Are foreign experts required to provide training for local consultants? ❑ Yes   ❑ No

II.4 Do you agree that over the last 5 years, the role share of local advisors and policymakers has increased relatively to the role of external advisors/assistance in formulating both the long and medium term plans/strategies? ❑ I agree ❑ I do not agree

II.5 Is training by foreign consultants of the local counterparts used as a measure of success of aid projects? ❑ Yes ❑ No

II.6 Is the participation of local intermediaries in the management/execution of aid projects used as a measure of success? ❑ Yes ❑ No

II.7 What other measures/indicators are used to determine the success of aid projects/programs? (List the most important five indicators)

II.8 As a proportion of total cost of TA projects, what is roughly spent on salaries and fees for foreign consultants?
❑ 25% or less ❑ 40% ❑ 50% ❑ 60% or more ❑ Other (specify)

II.9 Has this percentage decreased over the last five years? ❑ Yes ❑ No

II.10 How high is the level of salaries and fees of foreign consultants as a multiple of local fees?
❑ Twice as high ❑ Three times ❑ Four times ❑ More than four times ❑ Other (specify)

II.11 How high are salaries for local persons working in donor-assisted projects as a multiple of public-sector salaries?
❑ 20% higher ❑ 40% higher ❑ 60% higher ❑ More than twice as high ❑ Other (specify)

II.12 Does your experience confirm that the civil service is likely to witness any employment loss of best brains in favor of donor-assisted programs? ❑ Yes ❑ No

II.13 In your view, do you think that technical assistance has strengthened capacity building over the last five years? ❑ Yes ❑ No

Country-led Partnership

0. General

0.1 Has your organization accepted the CDF principle of partnership in aid relationships which is led by the recipient country? ❑ Yes ❑ No

0.2 Aside from the broad acceptance of the 'principle' to 'listen more to the recipients,' has your organization taken definitive steps in terms of changing the legal framework governing aid relationships? ❑ Yes ❑ No

0.3 When was the last change/ amendment to your institution's legal basis for or rules governing aid relationships? State Year and month of change

0.4 Please cite the relevant clause(s) that make the critical difference between the 'old' and the 'new' relationships:

0.5 Beside any changes in the laws governing aid, are there fundamental changes in the administrative rules and procedures governing development assistance in your organization that require recipient-driven ownership and partnership? ❑ Yes ❑ No

Comments:

0.6 Has there been any internal restructuring of your organization (downsizing or creation of new departments or institutional strengthening) to respond to the 'new' aid relationships?
❑ Yes ❑ No

Comments:

0.7 Are there examples of projects or programs which are currently being funded in a manner that reflects country ownership and recipient-driven partnership? ❑ Yes ❑ No

Comments:

1. Aid Coordination

1.1 Has aid coordination improved in the CDF countries after the introduction of the CDF/CDF-like principles? ❑ Yes ❑ No

Comments:

1.2 Has the division of labor increased among donors in the CDF countries? ❑ Yes ❑ No

Comments:

1.3 Are there effective government-led mechanisms for aid coordination in the CDF countries?
❑ Yes ❑ No

Comments:

1.4 Has your agency/organization over the last two years actively supported partner countries in strengthening their capacity to lead aid coordination? ❑ Yes ❑ No

Comments:

1.5 What are the reasons for lacking government-led aid coordination?
(Please rank the reasons below 1-5, where 5 gives the highest weight)

Constraints	*Rank*				
Lack of local institutional capacity	❏ 1	❏ 2	❏ 3	❏ 4	❏ 5
Government unwillingness to lead	❏ 1	❏ 2	❏ 3	❏ 4	❏ 5
Constraints on donors by their respective laws and procurement procedures	❏ 1	❏ 2	❏ 3	❏ 4	❏ 5
Donor preferences differ	❏ 1	❏ 2	❏ 3	❏ 4	❏ 5
Poor mechanism for donor coordination in the country	❏ 1	❏ 2	❏ 3	❏ 4	❏ 5

Comments:

1.6 Could closer alignment of donor and governmental priorities come at the expense of civil society-government relations in recipient countries? ❏ Yes   ❏ No

Comments:

2. Donor Harmonization

2.1 Are recipient countries playing any significant role in the harmonization efforts?
❏ Yes   ❏ No

Comments:

2.2 Is there any difference in harmonizing procedures with CDF countries compared to non-CDF countries? ❏ Yes   ❏ No

Comments:

2.3 Does donor headquarters policy hinder the development of country specific harmonization?
❏ Yes   ❏ No

Comments:

2.4 Do you undertake any joint monitoring and evaluation (with recipient governments) of development programs since the CDF was launched? ❏ Yes   ❏ No

Comments:

3. Nature of Aid - Aid Modalities

3.1 Has there been any movement in your aid program from project support to program and budget support over the last two years? ❏ Yes   ❏ No

Comments:

3.2 Do you use program aid more frequently in CDF countries compared to non-CDF countries? ❏ Yes ❏ No

Comments:

3.3 Do you foresee an increased delegation of authority and decentralization of staff to in-country offices in countries where you provide program aid ? ❏ Yes ❏ No

Comments:

3.4 Technical assistance often appears to be supply-driven, expensive and excessive, hampering true ownership and the use of local capacities. Have you changed the direction of your technical assistance program over the last two years? ❏ Yes ❏ No

Comments:

3.5 Do you support Project Implementation Units in the conduct of aid programs in the CDF countries? ❏ Yes ❏ No

Comments:

3.6 Have you replaced any own reporting requirements with regular government reports in any CDF country over the last two years? ❏ Yes ❏ No

Comments:

4. Policy Shifts among Donors/IFIs/Multilateral Organizations

4.1 Have you aligned your country assistance programs with the CDF countries' development strategies (PRSP)? ❏ Yes ❏ No

Comments:

4.2 Do you consult with the national Parliament in the recipient country when preparing your country assistance strategy? ❏ Yes ❏ No

Comments:

4.3 Has any steps been taken in your country to improve coherence among different policies affecting low-income countries, based on the poverty reduction objective? ❏ Yes ❏ No

Comments:

4.4 Will the implementation of Country-led Partnership principle result in lower transaction costs of aid programs? ❏ Yes ❏ No

Comments:

5. Partnership

5.1   What are the main obstacles to implement a country-led Partnership? Comments:

5.2   How can donors best promote country-led Partnership? Comments:

5.3   Given a willingness to listen more to the recipient country (being in the driver's seat) is partnership development contradictory to genuine ownership?   ❑ Yes   ❑ No

Comments:

5.4   Has the cooperation among different actors in your country (government, civil society organizations, private sector) increased with regard to your development assistance program as a result of the introduction of the CDF principles?   ❑ Yes   ❑ No

Comments:

5.5   Has your cooperation with different non-governmental actors (civil society, private sector) in the recipient country increased since the introduction of the CDF principles   ❑ Yes   ❑ No

Comments:

5.6   Is the implementation of the Partnership principle viewed by stakeholders in the recipient country as imposed by donors?   ❑ Yes   ❑ No

Comments:

5.7   Has the quality of partnership been negatively influenced by the extent of indebtedness and by aid dependency in the recipient countries?   ❑ Yes   ❑ No

Comments:

Results Orientation

1.   Has your organization done any of the following things to encourage aid recipients to adopt a "results orientation"? Please check all that apply.

❑ Required aid recipients to identify and track performance indicators;

❑ Called for plans that include performance indicators;

❑ Provided technical assistance to help a country and/or its local governments to develop a performance indicators process;

❑ Provided funds or other resources to the aid recipients for training in performance measurement and/or performance management;

❑ Other. (Please describe.)

❑ Have not attempted to encourage a results orientation.

2. What "results orientation" results do you believe have occurred? Please be as specific as possible. Please describe both results within specific projects and those in country development more generally.

3. Do you believe any problems have arisen because of different messages provided to aid recipients by donors as to what should be done to achieve a "results orientation"? ❑ Yes ❑ No

    If yes, please describe those problems.

4. Do you believe that any of the following problems have occurred in your organization's attempt to deliver "results orientation" messages to aid recipients? Please check all that apply.

    ❑ Lack of clear definitions of the key "results orientation" terms.

    ❑ Allocating too few resources to advance "results orientation."

    ❑ Not providing consistent aid for a sufficient amount of time.

    ❑ Not giving assisted countries enough time to implement the principles adequately; expecting too much too quickly.

    ❑ Conflicting objectives of donors

    ❑ Lack of coordination among donors

    ❑ Lack of interest/support by the assisted countries.

    ❑ Lack of assisted-country expertise to adequately implement the needed activities.

    ❑ Units within your organization not providing consistent messages.

    ❑ Lack of understanding within your own organization as to what "results orientation" is and how it should be promoted.

    ❑ Not adequately evaluating the progress your organization is achieving in a "results orientation" by countries you are assisting.

    ❑ Other. (Please describe.)

5. To what extent do you believe that the Millennium Development Goals/International Development Goals (MDG/IDG) will help assisted countries to improve development effectiveness:

    ❑ To a considerable extent

    ❑ To some extent

    ❑ Little, if any, effect

    ❑ Will have a negative effect

    ❑ Am not familiar with the MDG/IDG

Multi-Stakeholder CDF Evaluation Process: Analysis of Survey Questionnaire Results

Introduction

The following analysis synthesizes findings on the benefits and costs of the multi-stakeholder evaluation process to the members of the CDF Evaluation Steering Committee based on survey results from 10 representatives of 9 agencies. The questionnaire survey instrument is attached at the end of this analysis.

The response constitutes about 35 percent of the total number of entities (26) represented on the Steering Committee (SC). Established in January 2001, the SC included about 30 individual representatives from recipient countries, bilateral and multilateral donors, a nongovernmental organization (NGO), and two private sector firms.

SC member participation in the CDF evaluation has taken several forms:

- Membership on the Steering Committee

- Financial support

- Commenting on drafts by e-mail

- Formation of and/or participation in case study country "reference" groups and workshops, or assisting case study implementation in other ways (e.g., arranging meetings and interviews).

Design and Implementation of the CDF Evaluation

Survey respondents had mixed views on the extent to which their organizations had an influence on the *design* and implementation of the evaluation. Fifty percent of respondents (5 out of 10) felt they would have liked more opportunity to influence the design of the evaluation, while 60 percent (6 out of 10) felt they would have liked more opportunity to influence the *implementation* of the evaluation. One respondent expressed the view that although many of the Steering Committee members' comments, presented at various meetings, were taken into account in the Design Paper, some of the methodological problems identified at earlier stages still remained. Furthermore, the same respondent felt that once the evaluation started, few possibilities were given to Steering Committee members to affect the implementation of the evaluation. The Steering Committee meeting held in Kampala, Uganda, in January 2002 was the only meeting organized during the implementation process, during which very little time was devoted to discussing the Uganda report, precluding the possibility of affecting the implementation of subsequent country studies.

Only two respondents felt they had considerable opportunity to influence the design of the evaluation. But respondents felt they had relatively more opportunity at the implementation stage compared with the design stage; three respondents asserted many opportunities for influencing the evaluation's implementation.

Involvement in the CDF Evaluation

Since the launch of the CDF evaluation, there have been three official Steering Committee meetings, held in Copenhagen (Denmark), Kampala (Uganda), and Santa Cruz (Bolivia), in January 2001, 2002, and 2003, respectively. The majority of respondents, 60 percent (6 out of 10), found their participation in Steering Committee meetings to have been very useful, while the remaining respondents, 40 percent (4 out of 10), found it somewhat useful.

CDF evaluation documents and drafts (country case studies, thematic studies, Synthesis Report) have been regularly posted on the evaluation Web site, and 30 percent of respondents (3 out of 10) found their involvement in reviewing these materials to be very useful, while 40 percent (4 out of 10) found it to be somewhat useful. Two respondents of the Steering Committee felt that it was more trouble than it was worth. One respondent found the Web site to be a poor medium for triggering broader and better debate among Steering Committee members. Another felt that draft reports were not always available in time to give comments, limiting the Web site's usefulness as a channel for active involvement in the evaluation.

Only one respondent participated in a CDF evaluation mission and found it to be very useful. Six respondents participated in country workshops, with two of the respondents finding the workshops very useful, while three found them to be only somewhat useful. One respondent found the workshops not at all useful.

Four of the respondents had provided financial support to the CDF evaluation, and one found that mode of involvement very useful, while the other three found it to be only somewhat useful.

Impact of a Multi-Stakeholder Approach on the CDF Evaluation

Half of the respondents felt that the multi-stakeholder approach had a positive impact on the

diversity and quality of the evidence for the evaluation. Three respondents, however, had mixed views on the same dimension, with two respondents finding the approach to be largely positive, while one found it to be largely negative.

Respondents were almost equally divided on the impact of the multi-stakeholder approach on the quality of the analysis, with 40 percent (4 out of 10) finding the approach to have had a positive impact on the quality of the analysis, while another 50 percent (5 out of 10) felt it was mixed but largely positive. Similarly, 40 percent (4 out of 10) of the respondents felt the approach had a positive impact on the credibility of the findings, while another 40 percent held mixed views, with three respondents finding the approach to have had a largely positive impact, while one found it to have a largely negative impact.

The majority of respondents, 80 percent (8 out of 10), had mixed views on both the timeliness and the administrative costs of the evaluation. Fifty percent (5 out of 10) of respondents felt that the approach had a mixed but largely positive impact on the timeliness of the evaluation, while 20 percent (2 out of 10) felt it had a negative impact. Only one respondent was of the opinion that the approach had a positive impact on the timeliness of the evaluation. Similarly, 50 percent (5 out of 10) of respondents felt that the approach had a mixed but largely positive impact on the administrative costs of the evaluation, while 20 percent (2 out of 10) felt it had a largely negative impact. Only one respondent was of the opinion that the approach had a positive impact on the administrative costs.

Major Advantages of a Multi-Stakeholder Approach

Most respondents who answered this question (no. 4 in the attached questionnaire) see the diversity of the stakeholders that make up the Steering Committee as a major advantage, which assured that the Approach Paper for the evaluation would reflect a multi-perspective approach rather than a single-perspective approach. The diversity is also given credit for creating opportunities for consultations and comments and for stimulating debate, thereby increasing the quality of the analysis. Other stated advantages include:

- Diversity and credibility of evidence

- Relevance of issues to numerous development agencies

- Impact of evaluation findings if acted upon by development agencies

- Broadening of consensus

- Access to sources of information that no single agency could have

- Mix of quantitative and qualitative assessments

- Transparency of the process

- Role in the placement of a participatory monitoring system

- Help with the planning of new initiatives in the future.

Major Disadvantages of a Multi-Stakeholder Approach

Most respondents who answered this question (no. 5) felt that as the evaluation got under way, the participation of the different stakeholders was not mainstreamed, thereby garnering limited participation from members. Other stated disadvantages include:

- High transaction costs

- Time consuming

- Lack of focus and simplicity

- Complexity of management process

- Poor representation of domestic stakeholders (i.e., government, civil society, business sector) in the evaluation governance structure

- Inadequate triangulation and active search for alternative views.

Ways of Achieving the Advantages at Lower Cost

One respondent felt that the thematic studies should have been given less prominence, wondering to what extent they really added value to the fieldwork and to the combined knowledge of the teams that undertook the evaluation. Additional suggestions for lowering the cost of the evaluation include:

- Fewer formal meetings and more virtual meetings and/or video conferencing

- More participation by local evaluators

- More delegation to consultants.

Appropriateness of Methodological Tools

The few respondents who expressed their views on this issue found the methodological tools employed, particularly for evaluating country case studies, to be adequate. However, one respondent expressed that there was a major disconnect between the log frame methodology outlined in the Design Paper and the methodology utilized in the country case studies.

Respondents, however, found the methodology used for the cross-country econometric analysis to be inappropriate, specifically the proxy indicators chosen for the analysis.

One respondent was of the opinion that the case studies—some more than others—were thick with the opinion of the authors.

Questionnaire for Steering Committee Members on the Multi-Stakeholder CDF Evaluation Process

Given that the CDF evaluation has been a major multi-donor effort and that such evaluations are likely to increase in frequency, the stakeholders in this evaluation should have an opportunity to say what works and what doesn't.

Stakeholders involvement in the CDF evaluation has taken several forms:

- Membership on the steering committee

- Financial support

- Commenting on drafts via e-mail

- Participation (e.g., of a staff member) on country case study mission teams

- Formation of and/or participation in case study country "reference" groups and workshops.

We would like to get your views about the benefits and costs of the multi-stakeholder approach and the forms that your participation took.

There are seven questions in all; three that ask for ratings and four that are open-ended. Your answers will be recorded anonymously. Please submit only one set of answers for each participating government or organization.

1. To what extent did you (or your organization) have an opportunity to influence:

A. The design of the evaluation: (check appropriate answer)

❑ Considerably, amply

❑ Adequately

❑ Somewhat but would have liked more

❑ Not nearly enough

Comments:

B. The implementation of the evaluation: (check appropriate answer):

❑ Considerably, amply

❑ Adequately

❑ Somewhat but would have liked more

❑ Not nearly enough

Comments:

Please tell us about any specific kind of input that you or your organization would have liked to provide, but could not or were not able to? Why?

2. For you and your organization, how useful was each of these forms of involvement?

Participation in steering committee meetings

❑ Very useful

❑ Somewhat Useful

❑ Not useful

❑ More trouble than it was worth

❑ Didn't use this method

Review of documents/drafts on the Web site

❑ Very useful

❑ Somewhat Useful

❑ Not useful

❑ More trouble than it was worth

❑ Didn't use this method

Participation (e.g. by staff) in missions

❑ Very useful

❑ Somewhat Useful

❑ Not useful

❑ More trouble than it was worth

❑ Didn't use this method

Participation in country workshops

❑ Very useful

❑ Somewhat Useful

❑ Not useful

❑ More trouble than it was worth

❑ Didn't use this method

Financial support
- ❑ Very useful
- ❑ Somewhat Useful
- ❑ Not useful
- ❑ More trouble than it was worth
- ❑ Didn't use this method

Comments:

3. In your opinion, what impact did the multi-stakeholder approach have on the evaluation, along the four listed dimensions?

Diversity and quality of evidence
- ❑ Positive impact/improved
- ❑ Mixed but largely positive
- ❑ Mixed but largely negative
- ❑ Negative impact
- ❑ No impact either way

Quality of the analysis
- ❑ Positive impact/improved
- ❑ Mixed but largely positive
- ❑ Mixed but largely negative
- ❑ Negative impact
- ❑ No impact either way

Credibility of the findings
- ❑ Positive impact/improved
- ❑ Mixed but largely positive
- ❑ Mixed but largely negative
- ❑ Negative impact
- ❑ No impact either way

Timeliness/elapsed time of the evaluation
- ❑ Positive impact/improved
- ❑ Mixed but largely positive
- ❑ Mixed but largely negative
- ❑ Negative impact
- ❑ No impact either way

Administrative costs
- ❑ Positive impact/improved
- ❑ Mixed but largely positive
- ❑ Mixed but largely negative
- ❑ Negative impact
- ❑ No impact either way

Other (please state)
- ❑ Positive impact/improved
- ❑ Mixed but largely positive
- ❑ Mixed but largely negative
- ❑ Negative impact
- ❑ No impact either way

Comments:

4. What do you think were the major advantages, if any, of a multi-stakeholder approach?

5. What do you think were the disadvantages, if any, of the multi-stakeholder approach?

6. What might have been done differently to achieve the advantages at lower cost?

7. Did the CDF evaluation use the right methodological tools to answer the evaluation questions we set out to answer? If not, what should have been used?

Thank you for your inputs.
The Evaluation Secretariat

Endnotes

Chapter One

1. For a definition of development that includes much more than income levels, see Sen 1999. The annual UNDP *Human Development Reports* have also emphasized the broader dimensions of development.

2. Within a year after agreeing to have CDF implementation monitored for a pilot period, Jordan was dropped at its request.

3. The CDF Secretariat consists of nine World Bank staff members and is located in the Operations Policy and Country Services Vice Presidency.

4. The terms "framework" and "vision" require some clarification. As used in this evaluation, a vision becomes a framework when priorities are established for the elements of the vision. Therefore, the first CDF principle is called the Long-term, Holistic Development *Framework*. An alternative approach, adopted by the World Bank CDF Secretariat, is to refer to the principle as the Long-term, Holistic Vision.

5. Moreover, several donor countries have multiple agencies, each with their own procedures. Both bilateral and multilateral agencies are likely to be undercounted in table 1.2, since non-DAC donors are not included, and some multilateral agencies are undoubtedly missing.

6. *Poverty Reduction Strategy Papers—Operational Issues*, December 10 (1999); *The Poverty Reduction and Growth Facility (PRGF)—Operational Issues*, December 13 1999 (World Bank/IMF 1999a, b).

7. A chart, reproduced in Annex 4[B], shows the CDF as the overarching framework; the PRSP as the mechanism for articulating macroeconomic, social, and structural policies with the actions of all relevant stakeholders; and the various donor country strategies, such as the CAS, PRGF, and UNDAF, as the business plans that support it. This chart provides the clearest depiction of the PRSP as an action plan of the CDF.

8. In April 2000, the president of the Bank and the managing director of the IMF issued a joint statement on the relationship between the CDF and the PRSP. The statement synthesizes the basic principles of the CDF and shows the PRSP to be an operational vehicle based on it. It states that the CDF and the PRSP should be mutually reinforcing. See *The Comprehensive Development Framework (CDF)* and *Poverty Reduction Strategy Papers (PRSP)*, included as Annex 1.

9. In 2001 the Bank introduced the PRSC to support policy and structural reforms set out in the PRSP, complementing the PRGF's medium-term support of macroeconomic policies. The PRSC provides for the possibility of cofinancing with other donors, thus enhancing multidonor support for the PRSP.

10. The prospect of the PRSP serving as the sole basis for conditionality, however, is still remote. Even the more streamlined IMF PRGF still has separate performance criteria and benchmarks (although fewer than before), and conditions for HIPC completion include a number of other "triggers."

11. Under the Enhanced HIPC initiative, debt relief is delivered in two stages. At decision point, eligibility for assistance and for receipt of interim relief is established and requires an I-PRSP. The country receives the bulk of assistance at completion point, which requires one year's implementation of a full PRSP.

12. Twenty-two countries were brought to decision point in one year, compared with seven between 1998 and 1999.

13. This issue was raised by government representatives at the International Conference on national PRSPs in Washington, in January 2002. It has been acknowledged in "lessons for staff" in the recent Bank-Fund comprehensive review of the PRSP: *Review of the Poverty Reduction Strategy Paper Approach—Main Findings*, and *Review of the Poverty Reduction Strategy Paper Approach—Early Experiences with Interim and Full PRSPs* (World Bank 2002a).

14. See *External Comments and Contributions on the Joint Bank/Fund Staff Review of the PRSP Approach, Vol I: Bilateral Agencies and Multilateral Institutions; Vol II: Civil Society Organizations and Individual Contributions.* IMF/World Bank, January and February 2002 (World Bank 2002d, 2002e).

15. The PRSP was originally to be updated every three years. This corresponded with the three-year cycle of the PRGF, CAS, and PRSC. However, following the PRSP Review, there is now more flexibility about PRSP updating.

16. This appears to have improved Bank-Fund coordination on PRSP-related issues.

Chapter Two

17. Also allegedly never invited or underrepresented in PRSP processes are trade unions and women's organizations, as well as local governments in outlying areas. See Lister and Nyamugasira 2001.

18. The government of Uganda has internalized results orientation through its own poverty plan (the PEAP) and attendant M&E strategy. Chile has also developed a viable homegrown evaluation system. Brazil's emphasis on programs, clear goals/objectives, and performance indicators is very similar to the U.S. Government Performance and Results Act (GPRA).

19. For example, the macro data used in PRSPs and other strategic plans are often two or more years old.

20. Management notes that this is inconsistent with the CDF principles, which advocate regular and sustained stakeholder participation with strong links to institutions.

21. Evidence is largely drawn from two sets of survey questionnaires administered for the CDF evaluation (attached as Annex 6): (i) a survey on changes and trends in government-donor partnerships in five CDF case study countries—Bolivia, Ghana, Romania, Uganda, and Vietnam—that sought information on composition of donor portfolio, donor coordination, donor administrative and procedural requirements, and donor implementation practices (a total of 26 donors—17 bilateral and 9 multilateral—across the five countries that responded to the survey); and (ii) a structured survey questionnaire on the implementation of country-led partnership in the context of the CDF prepared as part of a thematic study, "Country-led Partnership." A total of 13 responses were received from the headquarters as well as country offices of six bilateral donors and one multilateral institution. For recipients' views, the findings of the six country case studies in the CDF evaluation have been drawn upon—Bolivia, Burkina Faso, Ghana, Romania, Uganda, and Vietnam. A reply was also received from the local World Bank team in Mozambique. For both donors and recipients, the sample is relatively small, but the responses are illuminating (see Holmgren and Soludo 2002, pp. 29-42).

22. Inference about progress depends largely on the country selection and the period covered by the study. For example, there are important differences between some of the survey results, the results summarized from the individual case studies for this CDF evaluation, and the summary of findings reported by an OECD study using a different set of 11 poor countries.

23. Forty-two of these countries are PRSP countries. World Bank. 2001a, pp. 13, 30-31.

24. It is likely that a number of these figures are underestimates. The Country Office of the World Bank in Romania reports that it received over 10 missions *per month* in the last quarter of calendar year 2002.

25. One factor that may account for this growth is increased emphasis by the OECD DAC Evaluation Working Party on joint evaluations, with the Evaluation Working Party serving as a point of coordination and follow-up for some efforts, such as a recent Joint Evaluation of the Education Sector in Bolivia. These data combine monitoring, supervision, and evaluation missions. There could be greater differences in each of the three components.

26. There remains a strong preference for separate missions in Ghana, partly due to a rise in donor competition and need/pressure for "attribution" and "planting the flag," as Ghana is once again emerging as an African success story.

27. Germany and Japan, for example. The United States Agency for International Development (USAID) is restricted by legislative provisions, particularly regarding sectoral priorities. Within these parameters, however, its local mission directors have considerable latitude to engage in harmonization efforts.

Chapter Three

28. These sectors have also been emphasized in HIPC programs. SWAps typically are constructed through participatory mechanisms, involve agreements between stakeholders (including donors) over objectives, activities and targets, pooled funding, and joint monitoring.

29. The MTEF provides aggregate and sectoral budget ceilings consistent with resource availabilities, typically over a three-year period on an annually rolling basis.

30. Uganda repackaged the PEAP summary as a PRSP to comply with the formalities. It had already received debt relief under the original HIPC initiative in 1998, and reached its decision and completion points under the Enhanced HIPC initiative in only two months.

31. Particular weaknesses were the selection of indicators and costings, which both tended to be left until the last minute.

32. In addition to country program efforts, particularly those supported through Poverty Reduction Support Credits (PRSCs), the World Bank and partner donors are supporting several PRSP-related capacity building programs, including the World Bank Institute "Attacking Poverty Program" and the PRSP Trust Fund.

33. The Bolivian PRSP consultation process had to be suspended in April 2000 when a state of siege was declared to suppress social protests.

34. The four indicators are measures of contract enforcement, credit markets, entry regulations, and labor regulations.

35. The ratings of policy and institutional quality are taken from the results of the Country Policy and Institutional Assessment (CPIA). The CPIA is an internal World Bank index of 20 equally weighted components. World Bank country specialists rate each component on a scale of 1-6, using standardized criteria. The components are grouped into four categories: (a) Macroeconomic management and sustainability of reforms; (b) Structural policies for sustainable and equitable growth, (c) Policies for reducing inequalities, and (d) Public sector management. Although the CPIA is an internal World Bank index, and is, therefore, subject to concerns about subjectivity and transparency, it is comprehensive and available for all recipient countries. A recent report by the World Bank's CDF Secretariat (2001a, p. 25) observes, "the CPIA process has recently being strengthened by improving its clarity and making its criteria more explicit by requiring a written explanation of each country's rating on each question, and implementing regular annual discussions with IDA recipient countries on the results for their country, thereby allowing the CPIA to be an input in the upstream dialogue with IDA countries." Further work has begun on better linking CPIA with CDF/PRSP processes, the Bank's country assistance strategy, and other economic and sector work.

36. This is a component index of the CPIA (see previous footnote).

37. It is argued that country-led partnership is likely to be higher, or at least the conditions for country-led partnership would be higher, for countries where most aid is provided by a few donors and is evenly distributed across many sectors, and technical assistance is not too high, relative to what is required for enhancing institutional capacity of these countries.

38. Limited data precluded using income inequality, though it is likely to generate similar results, as in the case of the growth literature (e.g., Rodrick 1999).

39. Similar results also obtain in analysis of cross-country growth regressions, where the negative marginal effect of ethnic fractionalization, estimated in this model, either disappears (e.g., Collier 2001), or is substantially reduced (e.g., Easterly 2000).

40. When the CPIA was regressed against these factors after it had been regressed against the CDF-like index (i.e., once the CDF-like index had been taken into account), it was found that the factors had no further influence (explanatory power) on the CPIA.

Chapter Four

41. Accession to the EU can serve this function to a certain extent, as it does in Romania. But there are limitations. As noted in the Romania case study, the EU does not attempt to harmonize policy in some sectors among its members (for example, health, education, and poverty), and therefore does not stress them in its requirements for accession. Romania seeks to link its new anti-poverty policy to the EU policy on social inclusion, but this is not a requirement for accession.

42. Among these donors are Denmark, the EC, Ireland, the Netherlands, Sweden, the U.K., and the World Bank. Performance of most donors varies from country to country.

43. See Eriksson and others 2002, Annex D-1, 2, and 4.

Annex Two

44. See the OED 1999 for an examination of the lessons of development experience through the lens of the CDF principles.

45. Documentation can be found on the CDF Evaluation Web site.

46. The term "development agencies" is used to mean official bilateral donors and multilateral development assistance organizations, as well as international NGOs.

47. As discussed at greater length below, the evaluation will seek complementarity and to avoid duplication with ongoing PRSP monitoring and evaluation efforts, such as those being undertaken under the auspices of the Strategic Partnership with Africa (SPA) and the U.N. Economic Commission for Africa (UNECA).

48. This does not preclude the possibility that, for example, country studies or the synthesis study would recommend that an independent panel to review donor performance be considered, but this should not be confused with the country studies themselves.

49. The IDGs call for the achievement of quantitative global goals in poverty reduction, infant and maternal mortality, primary and secondary education, access to reproductive health services, eliminating gender disparities, and environmental sustainability over the next 15 years.

50. The thematic studies will also include the experience of non-CDF pilot countries in their analyses but will not involve field work.

51. Members from the case study countries on the main steering committee will be asked to help identify members for each country steering committee and in the selection of the local institution.

52. The questions posed in the survey and interview protocols will include "core questions" developed in the evaluation Design Paper, but will also include country-specific questions proposed by the local steering committee and partner institution(s).

53. In-depth country case studies on PRSP implementation are being conducted in eight African countries under the auspices of the SPA. The countries are: Benin, Ghana, Kenya, Malawi, Mali, Mozambique, Rwanda, and Tanzania. The studies are being conducted by the Overseas Development Institute (ODI) in London, under the supervision of DFID. Preliminary reports are to be prepared by mid-2001. ODI, with DFID support, is also embarking on a PRSP monitoring effort. UNECA is establishing a "PRSP Learning Group" to provide a forum for exchange of views and experiences with the PRSP process among African countries. The CDF evaluation secretariat has initiated a dialogue with the managers of these efforts.

54. These considerations are discussed in two recent documents: Devarajan, Dollar, and Holmgren 2001; Collier and Dollar 2001.

55. Ultimate development impacts (e.g., life expectancy) are jointly determined by the adoption and implementation of the CDF principles as well as the intermediate outcomes and processes (e.g., expenditure programs, central bank independence, or extent of engagement of civil society). Intermediate outcomes/ processes, in turn, are also determined by the application of CDF principles.

56. In a paper prepared for the October 19-20, 2000 Workshop on the CDF Evaluation, John Williamson suggests that in these cases, "striking the right balance will involve recognizing (a) that there is room for professional disagreement even among those who share a common intellectual framework, and (b) that no one is omnipotent and there is often scope for extra ideas to be injected into the policy dialogue to mutual advantage" (Williamson 2000, p. 3).

57. This term and the set of issues it entails are discussed in Eriksson 2001, pp. 15-17.

Annex Four
58. Within a year after agreeing to have CDF implementation monitored for a pilot period, Jordan was dropped at its request.

Annex Five
59. These processes are outlined in the Design Paper for this evaluation (World Bank 2001c, pp. 10-11).

60. Polity IV code is a dataset users manual produced by the POLITY IV project. This project is part of the Integrated Network for Societal Conflict Research (INSCR) Program in the Center for International Development and Conflict Management (CIDCM) at the University of Maryland, College Park, MD.

61. The estimates for these a's are

$$I_{it} = -9.7991 + 0.1946T_{t-1} + 0.0993T_{t-1} \times I_{t-2} - 0.0125T_{t-1}^2 \times I_{t-2} + 1.5564LnY_{t-1} + 0.0129Sch$$
$$\quad\quad\quad (2.01) \quad\quad (2.34) \quad\quad\quad (-3.48) \quad\quad\quad (5.00) \quad\quad (3.27)$$

(t-values in brackets).

62. Our ICRG measure is a simple average of two ICRG measures of law and order, bureaucratic quality. Higher values of the measures denote better institutions.

Annex Six
63. The previous question asked about resource allocations/policy decisions. This one asks about results.

Bibliography

Ali, A., and A. Disch 2002. "On the Long-Term Holistic Development Framework Principle: An Evaluation." CDF Evaluation Secretariat, Operations Evaluation Department, World Bank, Washington, D.C.

Amis, P., and L. Green 2002. *Survey on Partners' Priorities and Perspectives on Harmonizing Donor Practices.* The University of Birmingham, U.K.: International Development Department, School of Public Policy.

Anderson, D., and others. 2002. *Ownership of SIDA Projects and Programs in East Africa: A Synthesis Report of Kenya, Tanzania, and Uganda.* Stockholm: Swedish International Development Authority.

Berg, Elliot. 1999. "Why Aren't Aid Organizations Better Learners?" Paper prepared for the Expert Group on Development Issues, Swedish Ministry of Foreign Affairs, Stockholm.

Boesen, Nils, Laura Kullenberg, José Antonio Peres A., and Juan Carlos Requena. 2002. *Bolivia CDF Evaluation Country Case Study.* CDF Evaluation Secretariat, Operations Evaluation Department, World Bank, Washington, D.C.

Boesen, Nils, Abena Oduro, Tony Killick, Laura Kullenberg, and Mirafe Marcos. 2002. *Ghana CDF Evaluation Country Case Study.* CDF Evaluation Secretariat, Operations Evaluation Department, World Bank, Washington, D.C.

Bonaglia, F., J. Braga de Macedo, and M. Bussolo. 2001. *How Globalisation Improves Governance.* OECD Development Centre Technical Paper No. 181. Paris.

Chapman, Jake. 2002. *Systems Failure: Why Governments Must Learn to Think Differently.* London: Demos.

CIDA (Canadian International Development Agency). 2002. *Canada Making a Difference in the World.* A Policy Statement on Strengthening Aid Effectiveness. Hull, Quebec.

Collier, Paul. 2001. "Implications of Ethnic Diversity." *Economic Policy* 5(32): 127-55.

Collier, Paul, and D. Dollar. 2001. "Development Effectiveness: What Have We Learned?" World Bank. Photocopy.

Collier, Paul, and Cathy Pattillo, eds. 1999. *Investment and Risk in Africa.* London: Macmillan.

Devarajan, S., D. Dollar, and T. Holmgren. 2001. *Aid and Reform in Africa.* Washington, D.C.: World Bank.

Disch, Arne, and Ali Abdel Gadir Ali. 2002. *On the Long-Term Holistic Development Framework Principle of the CDF: An Evaluation.* CDF Evaluation Secretariat, DECRG (Development Economics Research Group), World Bank, Washington, D.C.

Easterly, William. 2002. *The Cartel of Good Intentions: Bureaucracy versus Markets in Foreign Aid.* Working Paper No. 4. Washington, D.C.: Center for Global Development.

____. 2001. *The Elusive Quest for Growth: Economists' Adventures and Misadventures in the Tropics.* Cambridge, MA: MIT Press.

____. 2000. "Can Institutions Resolve Ethnic Conflict?" Photocopy.

Elbadawi, Ibrahim. 2001. "Social Cohesion, Conflict Management and Economic Growth in Africa." In T. Assefa, S. Rugumanu, and A. Ahmed, eds, *Globalization, Democracy, and Development in Africa: Challenges and Prospects.* Oxford, U.K.: African Books Collectives.

Elbadawi, Ibrahim, and Alan Gelb. 2002. "Financing Africa's Development: Toward a Business Plan." Paper presented at the AERC Senior Policy Seminar, Dar es Salaam, Tanzania.

Elbadawi, Ibrahim, George Mavrotas, and John Randa. 2003. *The Development Impact of CDF-like Experiences: An Assessment.* DECRG (Development Economics Research Group), World Bank, Washington, D.C.

Eriksson, John R. 2001. *The Drive to Partnership: Aid Coordination and the World Bank.* Operations Evaluation Department Study Series. Washington, D.C.: World Bank

____. 1999. *Aid Coordination: Moving Toward Partnership—The Challenge of Measurement.* Operations Evaluation Department. Washington, D.C.: World Bank.

Eriksson, John, David Pedley, Rosern Rwampororo, and Mirafe Marcos. 2002. *Uganda CDF Evaluation Country Case Study.* CDF Evaluation Secretariat, Operations Evaluation Department, Washington, D.C.

Eriksson, John, Lynn B. Salinger, Dumitru Sandu, and Manuela Sofia Stanculescu, 2002. *Romania CDF Evaluation Country Case Study.* CDF Evaluation Secretariat, Operations Evaluation Department, World Bank, Washington, D.C.

EC (European Commission). 2001. *Comparative Review of I-PRSP Targets and Conditionalities for HIPC Completion Point.* SPA Task Team on Contractual Relationships and Selectivity. Brussels.

____. 2000. *Review of Conditionalities Used for the Floating HIPC Completion Point.* SPA Task Team on Contractual Relationships and Selectivity. Brussels.

Evans, A. 2002. "Bank Strategy in Low-Income Countries: How Relevant and Effective Is the PRSP Process?" Poverty Reduction and Economic Management (PREM) Week. World Bank, Washington, D.C.

GAO (U.S. General Accounting Office). 1990. *Case Study Evaluations.* Washington, D.C.: GPO.

Gurr, Ted R. 1974. "Persistence and Change in Political Systems, 1800–1971." *The American Political Science Review* 68 (4): 1482-1504.

Hatry, Harry, and Kerfalla Yansane. 2002. *Comprehensive Development Framework Evaluation Results Orientation: An Early Look.* CDF Evaluation Secretariat, DECRG (Development Economics Research Group), World Bank, Washington, D.C.

Heimans, J. 2002. *Strengthening Participation in Public Expenditure Management: Policy Recommendations for Key Stakeholders.* Policy Brief No. 22, OECD Development Centre, Paris.

Helleiner, Gerry. 2000. *Toward Balance in Aid Relationships: Donor Performance Monitoring in Low-Income Developing Countries.* Prepared for a Festschrift in honor of Lance Taylor.

Herbst, J., and C. Soludo. 2001 *Aid and Reform in Nigeria.* In S. Devarajan and others, eds., *Aid and Reform in Africa.* Washington, D.C.: World Bank.

Holmgren, T., and C. Soludo. 2002. *Implementation of Country-Led Partnership in the Context of the Comprehensive Development Framework.* CDF Evaluation Secretariat, Development Research Group and Operations Evaluation Department, World Bank, Washington, D.C.

IMF/IDA (International Monetary Fund and International Development Association). 2002. *Review of the Poverty Reduction Strategy Paper (PRSP) Approach: Main Findings.* Washington, D.C.

Jerve, Alf Morten, Ray Mallon, Keiko Nishino, Han Manh Tien, and Laura Kullenberg. 2002. *Vietnam CDF Evaluation Country Case Study.* CDF Evaluation Secretariat, Operations Evaluation Department, World Bank, Washington, D.C.

Jolly, Richard, Giovanni Correa, and Frances Stewart, eds. 1987. *Adjustment with a Human Face.* New York: Oxford University Press.

Kanbur, R., T. Sandler, and K.M. Morrison, 1999. *The Future of Development Assistance: Common Pools and International Public Goods.* Overseas Development Council Policy Essay #25. Baltimore, MD: Overseas Development Council.

Lallement, Dominique, Della McMillan, Kyran O'Sullivan, Patrick Plane, and Kimsey Savadogo. 2002. *Burkina Faso CDF Evaluation Country Case Study.* CDF Evaluation Secretariat, Operations Evaluation Department, World Bank, Washington, D.C.

Lancaster, Carol, and Heba Handoussa. 2002. *Evaluating the CDF: Ownership and Participation*. CDF Evaluation Secretariat, DECRG (Development Economics Research Group), World Bank, Washington, D.C.

Lancaster, Carol, and Samuel Wangwe. 2000. *Managing a Smooth Transition from Aid Dependence in Africa*. Washington, D.C.: Overseas Development Council and the African Economic Research Consortium.

Lipumba, I.H. 2001 *Conditionality and Ownership: A View from the Periphery*. In *External Comments and Contributions on IMF Conditionality*. Washington, D.C.: IMF.

Lister, S., and W. Nyamugasira. 2001. *The Involvement of Civil Society in Policy Dialogue and Advocacy*. London: DFID.

Maxwell, S. 2003."Heaven or Hubris: Reflections on the 'New Poverty Agenda.'" *Development Policy Review* 21(1): 5-25.

Maxwell, S., and T. Conway. 2000. "Perspectives on Partnership." Operations Evaluation Department, World Bank, Washington, D.C.

Marshall, Monty G., and Keith Jaggers. 2000. "Polity IV Project: Political Regime Characteristics and Transitions, 1800–1999, Dataset Users' Manual." Center for International Development and Conflict Management, University of Maryland, College Park.

Ministry for Foreign Affairs, Sweden. 1999. *Making Partnerships Work on the Ground*. Workshop Report, Ulvsunda Castle. Stockholm.

O'Connell, S. A., and C. Soludo. 2001. "Aid Intensity in Africa." *World Development* 29(9):1527-52.

OECD/DAC (Organisation for Economic Cooperation and Development/Development Assistance Committee). 2001a. *DAC Guidelines on Poverty Reduction*. Paris.

_____. 2001b. *Task Force on Donor Practices: Progress Report*. Paris.

_____. 1999. *On Common Ground: Converging Views on Development and Development Cooperation at the Turn of the Century*. Paris.

_____. 1996. *Shaping the 21st Century: The Contribution of Development Co-operation*. Paris.

OED (Operations Evaluation Department, the World Bank). 1999. *1999 Annual Review of Development Effectiveness*. Washington, D.C.: World Bank.

Picciotto, Robert. 2001. *Development Cooperation and Performance Evaluation: The Monterrey Challenge*. Operations Evaluation Department, World Bank, Washington, D.C.

_____. 1998. *The Logic of Partnership: A Development Perspective*. Operations Evaluation Department, World Bank, Washington, D.C.

Rodrik, Dani. 1999. "Where Did All the Growth Go? External Shocks, Social Conflict and Growth Collapses." *Journal of Economic Growth* 4(4): 385-412.

Sen, Amartya. 1999. *Development as Freedom*. New York: Alfred A. Knopf.

Soludo, Charles. 2002. "Toward the Next Generation of Reforms of Aid Policies and Global Governance." Paper presented at the ADB/OECD Third International Forum on African Perspectives, Paris.

_____. 1998. *Monitoring Economic Performance in Africa: Toward the Construction of Performance and Policy Stance Indices*. A Methodological Note for the Construction of the UNECA Indices. Discussion Paper Series, ESPD/DPS/98/2. Addis Ababa, Ethiopia: UNECA.

Stiglitz, Joseph E. 1998. "Towards a New Paradigm for Development: Strategies, Policies and Processes." 1998 Prebisch Lecture, UNCTAD, October 19, 1998. Geneva.

UNCTAD (United Nations Conference on Trade and Development). 2002. *The Least Developed Countries Report 2002: Escaping the Poverty Trap*. Geneva.

United Kingdom. *Eliminating World Poverty: A Challenge for the 21st Century*. British Government White Paper (1997). London.

United Nations. 2001. *Road Map Towards the Implementation of the United Nations Millennium Declaration.* New York.

van de Walle, Nicolas, and Timothy Johnson. 1996. *Improving Aid to Africa.* ODC Policy Essay No. 21. Washington, D.C.: Overseas Development Council.

Williamson, John. 2000. "Country Ownership, Public Participation, and the CDF." Paper prepared for the 2000 Workshop on the CDF Evaluation, October 19-20. World Bank, Washington, D.C.

Wolfensohn, James D. 1998. "The Other Crisis." Address to Board of Governors, World Bank, Washington, D.C.

____. 1997. *The Challenge of Inclusion.* Annual Meetings Address. Hong Kong, China, World Bank.

World Bank/International Monetary Fund. 2002. *Review of the Poverty Reduction Strategy Paper (PRSP) Approach: Main Findings.* Washington, DC.

____. 2001. *Tracking of Poverty-Reducing Public Spending in Heavily Indebted Poor Countries.* Washington, D.C.

____. 1999a. *Poverty Reduction Strategy Papers—Operational Issues.* Washington, D.C.

____. 1999b. *The Poverty Reduction and Growth Facility (PRGF)—Operational Issues.* Washington, D.C.

World Bank. 2002a. *Review of the Poverty Strategy Paper Approach—Main Findings and Issues for Discussion.* International Conference on National PRSPs, Bank-Fund. Washington, D.C.

____. 2002b. *Roundtables on Latin American Middle-Income Country Experience.* The CDF Secretariat, Operations Evaluation Department, World Bank, Washington, D.C.

____. 2002c. *Review of the Poverty Strategy Paper Approach—Early Experiences with Interim and Full PRSPs.* International Conference on National PRSPs, Bank-Fund. Washington, D.C.

____. 2002d. *External Comments and Contributions on the Joint Bank/Fund Staff Review of the PRSP Approach. Vol. I: Bilateral Agencies and Multilateral Institutions.* International Conference on National PRSPs, Bank-Fund. Washington, D.C.

____. 2002e. *External Comments and Contributions on the Joint Bank/Fund Staff Review of the PRSP Approach. Vol. II: Civil Society Organizations and Individual Contributions.* International Conference on National PRSPs, Bank-Fund. Washington, D.C.

____. 2001a. *Comprehensive Development Framework: Implementation Experience in Low-and Middle-Income Countries.* The CDF Secretariat, Washington, D.C.

____. 2001b. *Comprehensive Development Framework: Meeting the Promise? Early Experience and Emerging Issues.* The CDF Secretariat, Washington, D.C.

____. 2001c. *Design Paper for a Multi-Partner Evaluation of the Comprehensive Development Framework.* CDF Evaluation Secretariat, Washington, D.C.

____. 2000a. *Comprehensive Development Framework: Country Experience, March 1999–July 2000.* The CDF Secretariat, Washington, D.C.

____. 2000b. *Annual Review of Development Effectiveness.* Operations Evaluation Department Study Series. Washington, D.C.: World Bank.

____. 2000c. JSA Guidelines at Annex II, PRSP. *Progress in Implementation, August 14* (EBS/00/167), Washington, D.C.

____. 2000d. *Can Africa Claim the 21st Century?* Washington, D.C.

____. 1999. *HIPC Initiative—Strengthening the Link between Debt Relief and Poverty Reduction.* Development Committee DC/99-24 (E). Washington, D.C.

____. 1996. *Access to Education and Health Care in Uganda.* Eastern Africa Department and Social Policy Department, Country Operations Division, Washington, D.C.

ISBN: 0-8213-5643-7